Chapter 1: Introduction to Robotics and Artificial Intelligence

History of Robotics

For centuries, humans have been fascinated with the idea of creating machines that can mimic their actions and behaviors. This curiosity has led to the development of robotics, which is the branch of science and technology that deals with the design, construction, operation, and application of robots. The history of robotics can be traced back to ancient civilizations, where automata and mechanical devices were created for entertainment and religious purposes. However, it wasn't until the industrial revolution in the 18th and 19th centuries that the foundation for modern robotics was established. With the invention of steam engines, mechanical looms, and other machines, the concept of automation started to take shape. In the early 20th century, the first modern robot was created by Czech playwright Karel Čapek in his play "R.U.R" (Rossum's Universal Robots). This introduced the term "robot" into our vocabulary, which comes from the Czech word "robota" meaning forced labor. However, it wasn't until the 1960s that the first industrial robots were developed, paving the way for the use of robots in manufacturing and other industries.

Since then, robotics has made significant advancements, with robots being used in various fields such as medicine, agriculture, space exploration, and even household tasks. As technology continues to advance, the possibilities for robotics are endless, and we are only scratching the surface of what robots can do.

Defining Artificial Intelligence

Artificial Intelligence, or AI, is a field of computer science that focuses on creating intelligent machines that can perform tasks that usually require human intelligence. The concept of AI can be traced back to ancient Greek myths of robots and automatons. However, it wasn't until the mid-20th century that significant developments in this field were made. In 1956, the development of the first AI program, the Logic Theorist, by Allen Newell, Herbert Simon, and J.C. Shaw, marked the beginning of AI as a separate field of study. Since then, AI has made remarkable progress, with advancements in areas such as natural language processing, robotics, and machine learning. One of the most widely used definitions of AI was given by computer scientist John McCarthy, who described it as "the science and engineering of making intelligent machines." However, there is no single agreed-upon definition of AI, as it encompasses a vast array of techniques and technologies.

Overview of Robotics and AI in Electrical Engineering

The field of electrical engineering has played a significant role in the advancements of robotics and AI. From the design of sensors and actuators to the development of control systems and machine learning algorithms, electrical engineering is crucial for the progress of these fields. In robotics, electrical engineers are responsible for creating reliable and efficient systems for robots to sense their environment, process information, and make decisions. They also play a vital role in the design and development of control systems for robots to execute specific tasks accurately and efficiently. In AI, electrical engineers work on developing algorithms that can learn from data, solve problems, and make decisions. They also use their expertise in signal processing and control systems to create intelligent systems that can perform complex tasks. The integration of robotics and AI in electrical engineering has opened up new and exciting possibilities for the development of intelligent machines. With the advancements in technology, the future of robotics and AI in electrical engineering is promising, and we can expect to see groundbreaking innovations in the coming years.

In this book, we will explore the fundamentals of robotics and AI for electrical engineers and delve into the various applications of these fields in different industries. With the rapid advancements in technology, it is essential for electrical engineers to stay updated and be at the forefront of these developments. So, let's embark on this journey of discovery together and unravel the world of robotics and artificial intelligence.

Chapter 2: Fundamentals of Robotics

Types of Robots

When we think of robots, we often imagine the humanoid machines portrayed in movies and TV shows. However, there are many different types of robots that serve diverse purposes and functions. From industrial robots that assist with manufacturing to surgical robots that aid in medical procedures, robots have become an integral part of our lives. One type of robot is the mobile robot, which is equipped with sensors and wheels or legs that allow it to move and navigate its environment. These robots are commonly used in the transportation and logistics industries, as well as for exploration and search and rescue missions. Another type of robot is the manipulator or industrial robot, which is designed to perform a specific task repeatedly. These robots are often found in factories, assembling products or performing other manufacturing tasks with precision and speed. Medical robots, also known as surgical robots, have become increasingly popular in the healthcare industry. These robots assist surgeons with procedures, offering greater precision and flexibility than traditional methods.

There are also autonomous robots, which are able to perform tasks without human intervention. These robots are commonly used in agriculture, delivering precision and efficiency to tasks such as harvesting and spraying crops.

Robot Components and Systems

To understand how robots work, it is important to examine their components and systems. At the core of a robot are its mechanical structure and power source, which provide the physical framework and energy for its movements. The mechanical structure may consist of arms, legs, or wheels, depending on the type of robot. Sensors are crucial components in a robot, providing it with information about its surroundings. Most robots are equipped with a variety of sensors, such as cameras, sonar, and touch sensors, which allow them to perceive and interact with their environment. Actuators are components that allow a robot to move its body parts. They convert energy from the power source into movement, allowing the robot to carry out tasks.

The control system is the brain of a robot, processing sensory information and making decisions based on that information. This system is often controlled by a computer, which uses algorithms and programming to guide the robot's actions.

Kinematics and Motion Control

Kinematics is the study of motion without considering its underlying causes. In robotics, this field is essential for understanding the movement of robots and how to control it. One key concept in kinematics is forward kinematics, which describes the relationship between a robot's joints and its position in space. This understanding is crucial for programming a robot's movements and controlling its motion. Motion control is the ability to govern and adjust a robot's movements. This is often achieved through a combination of sensors, actuators, and control systems. Motion control allows a robot to perform tasks with precision and accuracy, making it an essential aspect of robotics.

Through kinematics and motion control, robots are able to perform a wide range of movements and tasks. Whether it's a mobile robot navigating through a busy warehouse or a surgical robot assisting a skilled surgeon, these fundamentals are essential for the development and operation of robots.

In conclusion, the world of robotics is diverse and constantly evolving. From mobile robots to industrial manipulators, these machines have become an integral part of our lives, providing precision, efficiency, and convenience in various industries. Understanding the components and systems of robots, as well as the principles of kinematics and motion control, is crucial for their development and operation. As technology continues to advance, we can expect to see even more innovative and sophisticated robots that push the boundaries of what is possible.

So let us embrace the world of robotics and continue to explore the endless possibilities it has to offer. Who knows, one day you may even have your own personal robot assistant, making your life easier and more enjoyable. The future is bright for robotics and we can't wait to see what it holds.

Chapter 3: Fundamentals of Artificial Intelligence

The field of Artificial Intelligence (AI) has seen significant advancements in recent years, prompting many to believe that we are on the verge of a major technological breakthrough. As electrical engineers, it is essential to have a strong foundation in the fundamentals of AI in order to stay at the forefront of this rapidly evolving field. In this chapter, we will explore the basics of Artificial Intelligence, including its primary subfields of Machine Learning, Deep Learning, and Neural Networks. So, let's dive in and explore the fascinating world of AI!

Machine Learning

Machine Learning is a subset of AI that involves the development of algorithms and statistical models that enable computers to learn and improve from data without being explicitly programmed to do so. It is responsible for some of the most significant advancements in AI, including natural language processing, computer vision, and autonomous vehicles.

One of the key concepts of Machine Learning is the use of training data, which is used to train the algorithms and models to make accurate predictions or decisions. The more data the algorithm has to learn from, the more accurate its predictions will be. This is known as supervised learning, where the algorithm is given labeled data to learn from. Other forms of learning include unsupervised learning, where the algorithm must find patterns and relationships in unlabelled data, and reinforcement learning, where the algorithm learns through trial and error.

Deep Learning

Deep Learning is a subset of Machine Learning that is inspired by the structure and function of the human brain. It involves the use of multiple layers of neural networks to process and analyze data, making it popular for tasks such as speech recognition, image recognition, and translation.

One of the significant challenges in Deep Learning is the training process, which requires a considerable amount of computing power and vast amounts of data. However, with recent advancements in technology and the availability of massive datasets, Deep Learning has seen significant breakthroughs, leading to its widespread use in various applications.

Neural Networks

Neural Networks are a fundamental component of both Machine Learning and Deep Learning. They are computer systems that are inspired by the structure and functions of the human brain, consisting of interconnected nodes that work together to process and analyze data. There are several types of Neural Networks, including Feedforward Neural Networks, Convolutional Neural Networks, and Recurrent Neural Networks, each with its unique architecture and purpose. These networks have been used to achieve impressive results in areas such as image recognition, speech recognition, and natural language processing.

In addition to their use in AI, Neural Networks are also being heavily researched and utilized in other fields, such as medicine, finance, and engineering. They have been used to make accurate predictions, detect anomalies, and classify data, making them a powerful tool for data analysis and decision-making.

Applications of AI

The concepts of Machine Learning, Deep Learning, and Neural Networks have been instrumental in the development of various applications in the field of Artificial Intelligence. Some notable examples include Siri and Alexa for natural language processing, facial recognition software for security purposes, and self-driving cars for autonomous transportation.

In the field of electrical engineering, AI has been used in various applications, such as power system optimization, intelligent energy management systems, and predictive maintenance of electrical equipment. With the increasing use of renewable energy sources and the integration of smart technology in power systems, the use of AI is becoming crucial in ensuring efficient and reliable operation.

Conclusion

The fundamentals of Artificial Intelligence, including Machine Learning, Deep Learning, and Neural Networks, are essential for anyone looking to enter the field of electrical engineering. Their applications are becoming increasingly prevalent in our daily lives, and their potential is limitless. By having a strong foundation in these concepts, we can contribute to the advancement and development of this exciting field, shaping the future of technology. So, let's continue to learn and innovate in the fascinating world of AI!

Chapter 4: Sensing and Perception in Robotics

Sensors and Actuators

Sensors and actuators are the backbone of robotics, providing perception and action capabilities for a robot. Without them, a robot would be unable to interact with its environment and would not be able to perform its designated tasks. Sensors are devices that gather information from the environment and send it to the control system of the robot, while actuators are devices that allow the robot to physically interact with its surroundings based on the information received from the sensors. There are various types of sensors and actuators used in robotics, each with its unique capabilities and functions. Some of the common sensors used in robotics include proximity sensors, light sensors, touch sensors, and temperature sensors. These sensors provide different types of information about the robot's environment, such as the distance to an object, the amount of light in the surroundings, the presence of physical contact, and the temperature. Actuators, on the other hand, are responsible for the movement and manipulation of the robot. These devices can be categorized into two main types: physical actuators, which physically move or manipulate the robot, and logical actuators, which trigger a response in the robot's control system. Examples of physical actuators include motors, pneumatic cylinders, and hydraulic actuators, while logical actuators can be switches, relays, or microcontrollers.

In order for a robot to be effective, it is essential to have the right combination of sensors and actuators. This allows the robot to accurately perceive its environment and perform its tasks efficiently. Advancements in technology have led to the development of sophisticated sensors and actuators that are more accurate, reliable, and compact, making them suitable for a wide range of robotic applications.

Computer Vision

Computer vision is a crucial aspect of robotics, as it allows robots to interpret visual data from their environment. Just like how humans use their eyes to gather information, robots use cameras and other vision sensors to capture images and videos of their surroundings. This information is then processed and analyzed to provide valuable insights about the environment and its objects. One of the primary applications of computer vision in robotics is in navigation. By using cameras and vision sensors, robots are able to detect and recognize navigational markers or landmarks in their environment. This enables them to navigate and move autonomously without the need for human intervention. In addition, computer vision also plays a crucial role in object recognition and identification, which is essential for a robot to interact with its environment.

However, computer vision in robotics goes beyond just navigation and object recognition. It also has uses in other areas such as human-robot interaction, where robots use their vision capabilities to perceive and understand human gestures and movements. This allows for more natural and intuitive communication between humans and robots. Computer vision also has applications in quality control, where robots can detect defects or abnormalities in products during the manufacturing process.

Object Recognition

Object recognition is the process by which robots identify and classify objects in their environment. It involves using sensors and algorithms to analyze visual data and determine the shape, size, color, and other characteristics of an object. This information is then compared to a database of known objects for recognition. There are various methods and techniques used for object recognition in robotics, including feature extraction, edge detection, template matching, and neural networks. In recent years, there has been significant progress in this field, thanks to advancements in deep learning and artificial intelligence. This has allowed robots to not only recognize objects but also continuously learn and improve their recognition capabilities. Object recognition is crucial for a robot to perform its tasks effectively, especially in industrial and manufacturing settings. For example, in a warehouse, robots equipped with object recognition capabilities can identify and classify products, making the process of picking and packaging more efficient. In healthcare, robots can use object recognition to assist with medication administration, ensuring patients receive the correct medication.

In conclusion, sensing and perception in robotics are essential for the successful operation of a robot. With the advancements in technology and the development of more sophisticated sensors and algorithms, robots continue to become more intelligent and capable of functioning in various environments. The possibilities for robotics and object recognition are endless, and we can expect to see even more advancements in the future.

Chapter 5: Motion Planning, Path Planning, and Trajectory Generation

In the world of robotics and artificial intelligence, one of the key challenges is to create autonomous systems that are capable of navigating through complex environments with precision and efficiency. This requires not only the ability to sense and perceive the environment, but also to plan and control the motions of the robot. In this chapter, we will explore three important aspects of motion planning - path planning, trajectory generation, and motion planning algorithms.

Motion Planning

Motion planning involves the process of determining a sequence of actions that a robot needs to take in order to reach a desired goal location. This can be a challenging task, especially in complex and dynamic environments where there are multiple obstacles that the robot needs to avoid. In order to achieve successful motion planning, the robot needs to consider factors such as its current location, the goal location, and the environment it is operating in.

Traditionally, motion planning involved constructing a discrete representation of the environment and searching for a collision-free path. However, this approach is limited by the fact that it cannot handle continuous environments or dynamic obstacles. As a result, more sophisticated algorithms have been developed, such as probabilistic roadmaps (PRMs), rapidly-exploring random trees (RRTs), and artificial potential fields.

Path Planning

Path planning is a subset of motion planning, which involves determining a specific path for the robot to follow in order to reach its goal location. The path needs to take into account factors such as the motion constraints of the robot, the presence of obstacles, and the overall efficiency of the path. There are several algorithms used for path planning, such as Dijkstra's algorithm, A* search, and potential field methods.

An important aspect of path planning is ensuring that the chosen path is collision-free. This can be achieved through the use of sensors and perception algorithms to detect obstacles and adjust the planned path accordingly. Another key consideration in path planning is ensuring that the path is smooth and continuous, which can be achieved through the use of spline-based methods.

Trajectory Generation

Once a path has been planned, the robot then needs to generate a trajectory that will guide its actual motion. Trajectory generation involves determining the precise joint angles and velocities that the robot needs to follow in order to travel along the planned path. This is particularly important for robots with manipulators, as the trajectory needs to take into account the kinematics and dynamics of the robot in order to achieve accurate control. There are various methods for generating trajectories, such as spline interpolation, polynomial interpolation, and iterative approaches. The choice of method depends on factors such as the robot's motion constraints, the complexity of the planned path, and the desired level of accuracy. Additionally, trajectory generation needs to take into account factors such as obstacle avoidance, joint limits, and optimization of motion parameters.

Conclusion

Motion planning, path planning, and trajectory generation are crucial components of autonomous systems, as they enable robots to navigate through complex environments and perform tasks with precision and efficiency. As robotics and artificial intelligence continue to advance, there will likely be more sophisticated algorithms and techniques developed for these important aspects of motion planning. By understanding the principles and methods behind each of these components, we can continue to improve the capabilities of autonomous systems and further advance the field of robotics.

Chapter 6: Simultaneous Localization and Mapping (SLAM)

The concept of localization and mapping is crucial for the development of autonomous robots. Without the ability to accurately perceive and understand their surroundings, robots would not be able to navigate and complete tasks in the real world. This is where Simultaneous Localization and Mapping (SLAM) comes in

- a technology that combines the abilities of mapping and localization into one simultaneous process. In this chapter, we will explore the fundamentals of SLAM and its role in advancing robotics and artificial intelligence.

Mapping Techniques

Mapping is the process of creating a representation or model of a physical environment. In the context of robotics, mapping refers to building a digital map of the robot's surroundings. This map allows the robot to understand its environment and navigate through it. Traditional mapping techniques involved manually creating maps through surveys and measurement. However, with advancements in technology and robotics, mapping techniques have become more efficient and accurate. One of the main techniques used for mapping in SLAM is simultaneous localization and mapping or feature-based SLAM. It involves processing sensor data from cameras, lidar, or other range sensors to identify and match features in the environment, such as corners and edges. These features are then used to build a map of the environment, allowing the robot to navigate and localize itself in real-time.

Another popular technique is occupancy grid mapping, which uses a grid-based representation of the environment. It divides the environment into smaller cells and estimates the probability of each cell being occupied by an obstacle. This technique is commonly used in mobile robotics for obstacle detection and navigation.

Localization Technologies

Localization is the process of determining the robot's position and orientation in a given environment. With the help of localization, the robot can accurately navigate and complete tasks in its surroundings. In SLAM, localization is achieved simultaneously with mapping, making it an essential component for creating a real-time map of the environment. One of the most widely used localization technologies in SLAM is the Global Positioning System (GPS). It uses satellite signals to determine the robot's position on Earth with high accuracy. However, GPS can be unreliable in indoor environments or areas with limited satellite coverage, making it ideal for outdoor use. Another localization technology is Visual Odometry (VO), which uses cameras to estimate the robot's position by tracking visual features in the environment. This technology is particularly useful in areas where GPS signals are weak or unavailable, such as indoor spaces or underground tunnels.

Sensor Fusion is another important technology for localization in SLAM. It involves combining data from multiple sensors, such as cameras, lidar, and inertial measurement units (IMU) to improve accuracy and reliability. By incorporating different types of sensors, the robot can have a more comprehensive understanding of its environment and its own position within it.

Rise of SLAM in Robotics and AI

Simultaneous Localization and Mapping has revolutionized the field of robotics and artificial intelligence. With SLAM technology, robots are now able to perceive and understand their surroundings without the need for pre-existing maps or GPS signals. This has paved the way for the development of more advanced and autonomous robots that can successfully operate in real-world environments. SLAM technology is widely used in various industries, such as transportation, agriculture, and healthcare. Autonomous cars use SLAM for navigation and obstacle detection, while drones use it for precise mapping and delivery. In agriculture, SLAM is used to map and monitor fields for efficient crop management. In healthcare, SLAM is used for precise navigation of medical robots during surgeries.

Additionally, advances in SLAM technology have also contributed to the development of self-driving cars and intelligent robots. With the help of deep learning algorithms and neural networks, robots are now able to continuously improve their mapping and localization capabilities, making them more efficient and accurate in their tasks.

The Future of SLAM

As technology continues to advance, we can expect to see even more sophisticated and reliable SLAM systems in the future. With the increasing demand for autonomous and intelligent robots, SLAM will play a crucial role in their development. We can also expect to see further integration of SLAM with other technologies like Artificial Intelligence, which will enhance the robots' decision-making capabilities and allow them to adapt to changing environments. Furthermore, the application of SLAM will expand beyond traditional industries, leading to new and innovative uses. From search and rescue missions to space exploration, SLAM technology will continue to push the boundaries of what is possible with robotics and artificial intelligence.

In conclusion, Simultaneous Localization and Mapping (SLAM) is an essential technology for the development of autonomous robots. Its ability to simultaneously map and localize is crucial for robots to perceive and understand their surroundings, enabling them to navigate and complete tasks in real-time. With the continuous advancements in SLAM, we can expect to see even more remarkable uses of robotics and AI in the future.

Chapter 7: Human-Robot Interaction

The advancement of technology has led to an increase in the use of robots in various industries and social settings. From manufacturing and healthcare to personal assistants and entertainment, robots have become an integral part of our lives. However, with this increased interaction between humans and robots, new challenges and opportunities have emerged.

Social Human-Robot Interaction

Social human-robot interaction refers to the interaction between humans and robots in social settings such as homes, schools, and public spaces. With the development of more human-like robots, the concept of social robots has gained popularity. These robots are designed to interact with humans in a more natural way, using gestures, speech, and facial expressions. One of the main advantages of social robots is their potential to assist humans in various tasks, such as providing companionship for the elderly or supporting children with special needs. These robots can be designed to understand human emotions and respond accordingly, creating a more personalized and human-like interaction.

Moreover, social human-robot interaction has the potential to bridge the gap between different cultures and languages, as robots can be programmed to communicate in various languages and have the ability to understand cultural nuances. This can promote a sense of cultural understanding and improve communication between people from different backgrounds.

Industrial Human-Robot Collaboration

Industrial human-robot collaboration involves the interaction between humans and robots in manufacturing and industrial settings. With the development of advanced robotics and artificial intelligence, collaborative robots, also known as cobots, have emerged. These robots are designed to work alongside humans, assisting them with various tasks and taking on physically demanding or dangerous tasks. The integration of cobots in industrial settings has shown significant improvements in efficiency and productivity. With the ability to work 24/7, these robots can help reduce human error and increase the speed and precision of production processes. This not only benefits the companies but also improves the working conditions for human employees.

An important aspect of industrial human-robot collaboration is safety. As humans and robots work in close proximity, it is crucial to have strict safety protocols in place to prevent any accidents or injuries. The development of advanced sensors and algorithms allows for real-time monitoring and detection of potential hazards, ensuring the safety of all individuals in the workspace.

Safety Considerations

Safety is a critical aspect of human-robot interaction, whether it is in social or industrial settings. As robots become more advanced and integrated into our daily lives, ensuring their safety and the safety of those around them is of utmost importance. Robots must be designed and programmed with safety in mind. This includes implementing proper risk assessment measures during the development stage and incorporating safety features such as emergency stop buttons and sensors that can detect and respond to human presence. Moreover, training programs for both humans and robots are essential for safe and efficient collaboration. Humans must be educated on how to interact with robots and handle them in various situations to prevent any accidents. On the other hand, robots must be programmed with specific behavior and protocols to ensure they do not cause harm to humans. Another critical consideration is the ethical implications of human-robot interaction. As robots become more human-like and integrated into our lives, questions arise regarding their autonomy and responsibility. Guidelines and regulations are necessary to address these ethical concerns and ensure ethical and responsible use of robots in society.

In conclusion, human-robot interaction is an exciting and rapidly evolving field. From social to industrial settings, robots have the potential to enhance our daily lives and improve productivity. However, it is crucial to consider safety, ethical implications, and proper training for humans and robots to ensure a harmonious and beneficial relationship between the two. With continued advancements in technology, the future of human-robot interaction looks bright, and we can expect to see even more sophisticated and useful robots in the years to come.

Chapter 8: Mobile Robotics

Mobile robots, also known as autonomous robots, are advanced machines designed to move around and complete tasks without human intervention. They are equipped with various sensors, actuators, and programmed algorithms to navigate and interact with their environment. Mobile robotics is a rapidly growing field, with applications in industries such as manufacturing, logistics, healthcare, and agriculture. In this chapter, we will explore the navigation, localization, control, and various applications of mobile robots.

Navigation

Navigation is the ability of a mobile robot to move from one location to another in its environment. This is a crucial aspect of mobile robotics, as it allows robots to complete tasks and interact with their surroundings. Navigation can be achieved through various methods, including:

- Odometry: This method involves using wheel encoders to track the movement of a robot and estimate its position and orientation. It is a simple and low-cost navigation method but is prone to error due to factors such as wheel slippage.

- Inertial navigation: By using inertial measurement units (IMUs) that consist of gyroscopes and accelerometers, robots can track their position and orientation based on changes in velocity and direction. This method is often used in conjunction with other navigation methods for better accuracy.

- Mapping: Robots can create maps of their environment using sensors such as LiDAR, cameras, and depth sensors. By comparing and aligning their current position with the map, robots can navigate and avoid obstacles.

- SLAM (Simultaneous Localization and Mapping): This approach combines mapping and localization to simultaneously build a map of an unknown environment and determine a robot's position within it.

Localization

Localization is the process of determining a robot's position and orientation within its environment. It is a crucial step in navigation and is essential for robots to accurately move and interact with their surroundings. Localization can be achieved through the following methods:

- GPS (Global Positioning System): By using satellite signals, robots can determine their position on a global scale. However, GPS is prone to inaccuracy and does not work well indoors.

- Beacons: Ultrasonic, infrared, or radio beacons can be placed in an environment to help robots localize themselves. The robot uses the beacon signals to determine its position and orientation.

- Visual odometry: By using cameras and image processing techniques, robots can determine their position by tracking visual features in their environment.

- Sensor fusion: This method combines data from multiple sensors, such as odometry and mapping, to improve localization accuracy.

Control in Mobile Robots

Control is the process of directing the movement of a robot to complete a task. It involves the use of algorithms based on sensor data to make decisions and adjust the robot's movements. There are two main types of control in mobile robots: open-loop and closed-loop.

- Open-loop control: This type of control involves pre-programmed movements and does not take sensor feedback into account. It is simple and fast but is not suitable for complex tasks.

- Closed-loop control: Here, the robot receives feedback from sensors and adjusts its movements accordingly. This type of control is more precise and can handle a variety of tasks.

With advances in artificial intelligence and machine learning, control in mobile robots is becoming more efficient and autonomous. Robots can learn from their environment and make decisions based on sensory data, making them more adaptable to changing environments.

Applications of Mobile Robots

The use of mobile robots is widespread in various industries and continues to grow as technology advances. Some of the common applications include:

- Warehousing and logistics: Mobile robots are used in warehouses to retrieve items and autonomously transport them to designated areas. This improves efficiency and reduces the need for human labor.

- Manufacturing: With the ability to move heavy objects and perform repetitive tasks with precision, mobile robots are extensively used in manufacturing industries.

- Healthcare: Mobile robots are used to transport medical supplies, assist with surgeries, and provide support in patient care.

- Agriculture: In the agriculture industry, robots are used for tasks such as planting, harvesting, and monitoring crops. They can operate in harsh environments and can work continuously without tiring.

- Education: Mobile robots are used in educational settings to teach students about robotics, coding, and problem-solving. They allow for hands-on learning and can spark interest in STEM fields.

In addition to these applications, mobile robots are also used in search and rescue operations, space exploration, and household chores. As technology advances and robotics becomes more accessible, the potential for mobile robots in various industries will continue to grow.

In Conclusion

Mobile robotics has come a long way, and with advancements in technology, the possibilities for its use are endless. Whether it is navigating through a warehouse or assisting with surgeries, mobile robots are transforming industries and making tasks more efficient. With further research and development, we can expect to see even more sophisticated and versatile mobile robots in the future. As such, the field of mobile robotics holds immense potential and opportunities for aspiring engineers to be a part of its growth and innovation.

Chapter 9: Autonomous Systems

Autonomous Vehicles

As technology advances, the dream of self-driving cars becomes a reality. Autonomous vehicles, also known as self-driving cars, are vehicles that can navigate and operate without human input. These vehicles use a combination of sensors, cameras, and artificial intelligence to detect and respond to their surroundings. The development of autonomous vehicles has the potential to revolutionize transportation, making it safer, more efficient, and accessible to all. One of the major benefits of autonomous vehicles is increased safety. Human error is responsible for the majority of car accidents, but with self-driving cars, the risk of accidents caused by distractions, drowsiness, or human error decreases significantly. Also, autonomous vehicles can constantly communicate with each other, reducing the probability of collisions. This technology has the potential to save thousands of lives every year. Another advantage of autonomous vehicles is increased efficiency. With self-driving cars, traffic flow can be optimized, reducing travel time and fuel consumption. These cars can react quickly to changes in traffic conditions and choose the most efficient routes. This not only saves time but also reduces carbon emissions, making our roads greener.

In addition to personal transportation, autonomous vehicles can also have a big impact on public transportation. Self-driving buses and shuttles can provide affordable, safe, and efficient transportation options for those who do not have access to a personal vehicle. With the use of artificial intelligence and data analysis, public transportation services can be tailored to the needs of the community, providing a more reliable and accessible transportation system.

Autonomous Drones

Drones, also known as unmanned aerial vehicles (UAVs), are becoming increasingly popular in various industries. These flying machines can be remotely controlled or operate autonomously, making them versatile tools for a wide range of applications. They have been used in the military, but now their potential in civilian use is being explored. Autonomous drones have the ability to fly pre-programmed routes, navigate through obstacles, and perform tasks without human intervention. This makes them useful for tasks such as surveying, mapping, delivery, and more. One of the main advantages of autonomous drones is their precision and accuracy. These machines can fly over difficult terrain, reach remote areas, and gather data that would be difficult or dangerous for humans to obtain. They can also perform tasks with precision, such as crop spraying or inspecting power lines. Additionally, autonomous drones can help reduce costs for various industries. Due to their ability to fly without human supervision, they can work longer hours and save on labor costs. They can also cover large areas more efficiently, reducing time and resources needed for tasks such as search and rescue or surveillance.

As technology continues to advance, the potential uses for autonomous drones will only expand. From delivering packages to monitoring traffic, these flying machines are becoming an essential tool for various industries, making tasks safer, more efficient, and cost-effective.

Robotics in Space Exploration

Since the first robots were sent into space in the 1960s, they have become vital tools for space exploration. These robots, also known as space probes, have the ability to navigate and conduct experiments without the need for human intervention. With the rapid advancement of robotics and artificial intelligence, we are now able to send more sophisticated machines into space, expanding the scope of our explorations. One of the key benefits of using robots for space exploration is their versatility. They can be equipped with different instruments and sensors, allowing them to collect data and perform tasks on different planets, moons, and other celestial bodies. They can also withstand harsh environments, such as extreme temperatures and radiation, which makes them ideal for space exploration. Robots are also able to conduct tasks more efficiently and safely than humans. With the risk of human life removed, these machines can explore areas that would be too dangerous for humans, such as the surface of Mars or the depths of the ocean on other planets. They can also work for longer periods of time without the need for rest or food, providing a continuous stream of data and information. Furthermore, using robots for space exploration can significantly reduce costs. Launching and maintaining human missions in space is incredibly expensive, but using robots can cut down on these costs significantly. This allows for more frequent missions and more opportunities for discoveries and research.

In the future, we can expect to see even more advanced robots being used for space exploration, potentially even opening up the possibility for human colonization of other planets. As technology continues to progress, the possibilities for robots in space exploration are limitless.

Conclusion

The use of autonomous systems, whether in the form of vehicles, drones, or robots, is reshaping our world in various ways. These machines offer increased efficiency, safety, and versatility in numerous industries, making tasks easier and more accessible. As we continue to explore the possibilities of robotics and artificial intelligence, the future looks bright for this innovative technology. With the proper regulations and ethical considerations, autonomous systems have the potential to make our lives better and take us to new frontiers.

Chapter 10: Kinematics, Dynamics, and Control of Robot Arms

Robot arms are a crucial part of any robotic system, allowing for precise movements and actions to be performed. In this chapter, we will delve into the fascinating world of robot arm kinematics, dynamics, and control. Through the use of mathematics and advanced engineering principles, we will explore the inner workings of these versatile and essential tools in robotics.

Kinematics

Kinematics is the study of the motion and position of objects without consideration of the forces causing the motion. In the case of robot arms, kinematics focuses on the geometry and movement of the arm itself, without taking into account the external forces acting on it. This branch of mechanics is essential in understanding how the joints of a robot arm move and how the end effector, or the tool attached to the end of the arm, can be controlled. Robot arms are typically made up of several revolute joints, which allow for rotational movement, and prismatic joints, which allow for linear movement. Through the use of trigonometry and coordinate systems, the position and orientation of these joints can be precisely calculated and controlled. For example, a two-link robot arm can be described using a set of equations called the Denavit-Hartenberg parameters, which take into account the lengths and angles of each link. There are also several different kinematic configurations, or movement patterns, that robot arms can have. The most common one is the serial configuration, where the links are connected end-to-end, allowing the arm to have a limited range of motion. Other configurations include the parallel configuration, where the arms are connected in a parallel arrangement, and the articulated configuration, where the links are connected through a series of joints with a larger range of motion.

Dynamics

Dynamics is concerned with the forces and torques that act on an object and how they affect its motion. In the case of robot arms, dynamics plays a crucial role in understanding the forces that need to be applied to the arm to achieve a desired movement or action. This includes not only the forces acting on the arm itself but also the external forces caused by the weight of the end effector and any objects it may be holding. Robot arms need to be designed not only to withstand these forces but also to use them efficiently. This involves carefully selecting the materials and motors used in the arm, as well as considering the weight and center of gravity of the end effector. By understanding the dynamics of a robot arm, engineers can optimize its design for maximum efficiency and accuracy. One especially important aspect of dynamics in robot arms is inverse dynamics. This involves calculating the forces and torques needed to achieve a desired motion or trajectory of the arm. By using mathematical models and simulations, engineers can determine the exact amount of force needed at each joint to move the arm in a specific manner.

Control of Robot Arms

Control is crucial in any robotic system, and robot arms are no exception. The control of robot arms involves using sensors, actuators, and algorithms to guide and adjust the movement of the arm to achieve a desired task. There are several types of control in robot arms, including open-loop, closed-loop, and feedback control. Open-loop control involves setting predetermined movements or trajectories for the robot arm without actively monitoring the arm's position or adjusting for any external forces. Closed-loop control, on the other hand, involves using sensors to monitor the position and movement of the arm and adjusting the control commands accordingly. This allows for more precise movements and adjustments to be made during operation. Feedback control, often used in combination with closed-loop control, involves continuously monitoring the performance of the robot arm and making adjustments to the control commands to improve its accuracy and efficiency. This is especially important in tasks that require a high level of precision, such as in manufacturing or surgery. With advancements in technology, many robot arms are now equipped with artificial intelligence and machine learning algorithms, allowing them to adapt and learn from their environment. This allows for even more complex movements and control of the arm, making them even more versatile in various industries.

End Effectors

An end effector is the tool or device attached to the end of a robot arm that allows it to interact with the environment. This can include grippers, welding torches, and sensors, to name a few. End effectors are an essential part of a robot arm, as they determine the tasks it can perform and the type of control and movement required. End effectors can range from simple grippers to more complex, specialized tools. For example, in the manufacturing industry, robot arms may use end effectors with suction cups or vacuum grippers to pick up and manipulate objects. In the medical industry, specialized end effectors such as scalpel holders or microsurgical tools may be used for delicate procedures. Designing and integrating end effectors with robot arms requires a deep understanding of the task at hand and the environment in which the arm will be operating. The right choice of end effector can greatly improve the efficiency, accuracy, and versatility of a robot arm, allowing it to perform a wide range of tasks.

In conclusion, the kinematics, dynamics, and control of robot arms play a crucial role in the design and operation of these versatile tools. Through a combination of mathematics, engineering principles, and advanced technologies, engineers are constantly pushing the boundaries of what robot arms can achieve. As robotics and artificial intelligence continue to advance, the possibilities for robot arms are limitless.

Chapter 11: Multiple Dimensions in Robotics: Multi-Robot Systems, Swarm Robotics, and Coordination and Control in Distributed Robots

As technology advances at a rapid pace, the field of robotics has been making huge strides, leading to the development of more sophisticated and intelligent machines. One of the most exciting and promising areas of research in robotics is the use of multiple robots to perform tasks efficiently and effectively. In this chapter, we will dive into the world of multi-robot systems, swarm robotics, and coordination and control in distributed robots, and explore the opportunities and challenges they present in the field of robotics.

Multi-Robot Systems

In traditional robotics, a single robot is typically designed to perform a specific task on its own. However, with the advancement in technology and the need for more complex and challenging tasks to be performed, the concept of multi-robot systems has emerged. Multi-robot systems can be defined as a group of robots that work together towards achieving a common goal or objective. The potential benefits of using multi-robot systems are numerous. These systems have the ability to improve efficiency, increase productivity, and reduce costs. Additionally, multi-robot systems can also effectively perform tasks that are too dangerous, difficult, or time-consuming for a single robot to handle on its own. This makes them ideal for use in various industries such as manufacturing, agriculture, medicine, and even space exploration.

Swarm Robotics

Swarm robotics is a subset of multi-robot systems that takes inspiration from the behavior of social insects, such as ants, termites, and bees. In nature, these creatures work together in large groups to accomplish complex tasks, such as building elaborate nests and foraging for food. Similarly, swarm robotics involves the coordination and control of a large number of simple robots to perform tasks in a collaborative manner.

One of the biggest advantages of swarm robotics is its ability to adapt and respond to changing environments. As each robot in the swarm has limited capabilities, the failure of one or even several robots will not affect the overall performance of the system. This makes swarm robotics a highly resilient and robust solution for various applications, including search and rescue, environmental monitoring, and military surveillance.

Coordination and Control in Distributed Robots

Coordination and control are vital components of any multi-robot system. In a distributed robot system, the individual robots have to work together efficiently and effectively. This requires a sophisticated coordination and control mechanism that enables robots to communicate, share information, and make decisions. One of the key challenges in achieving coordination and control in distributed robots is the issue of scalability. As the number of robots in the system increases, the complexity of coordinating their actions and behaviors also increases. To address this challenge, researchers are exploring different approaches, such as decentralization, where robots make decisions autonomously, and centralization, where a single entity controls the entire system.

Opportunities and Challenges

The use of multiple robots in different applications opens up a world of opportunities. From improving efficiency and reducing costs in industries to facilitating disaster relief and space exploration, multi-robot systems have the potential to make a significant impact on our lives. However, with these opportunities come challenges, such as designing efficient coordination and control algorithms, managing communication and information sharing between robots, and dealing with the issue of scalability. As the field of robotics continues to advance, it is evident that multi-robot systems, swarm robotics, and coordination and control in distributed robots will play a crucial role in shaping the future of technology. With ongoing research and development, we can expect to see even more sophisticated and intelligent robots that work together seamlessly to achieve greater efficiency and productivity.

The Future is Multi-Dimensional

In conclusion, the use of multiple robots to accomplish complex tasks is no longer just a concept, but a reality. Multi-robot systems, swarm robotics, and coordination and control in distributed robots are revolutionizing the field of robotics and paving the way for a more multi-dimensional future. As researchers continue to push boundaries and explore new ways of utilizing robots, we can only imagine the endless possibilities that lie ahead. What excites us the most is the potential for these advancements to benefit society and make our lives easier, safer, and more comfortable. The future is indeed multi-dimensional, and it is an exciting time to be a part of the journey towards it.

Chapter 12: Design and Development of Humanoid Robots

Humanoid Robot Design

When it comes to robots, the term "humanoid" refers to robots that are built to resemble humans in shape and appearance. While many robots have been designed with a more utilitarian look, humanoid robots have captured the imagination of scientists and engineers with their anthropomorphic features and abilities to mimic human movements. Creating a humanoid robot involves a combination of engineering, computer science, and art. The design process starts with the decision of what features and abilities the robot will have, such as its height, number of limbs, and sensors. The appearance of the robot is also carefully crafted, often taking inspiration from human anatomy and aesthetics. One of the key challenges in humanoid robot design is creating a balance between the robot's appearance and its functionality. Since humanoid robots are expected to perform tasks in environments designed for humans, their design must allow for smooth locomotion, manipulation of objects, and human-like movements. Another consideration in designing humanoid robots is the materials used. Most humanoid robots are made of lightweight and durable materials, such as aluminum, titanium, and carbon fiber, to allow for efficient and flexible movement. The use of lightweight materials also reduces the strain on the robot's motors, increasing its energy efficiency and overall performance.

In addition to the physical design, humanoid robots also require sophisticated software and hardware systems to control their movements. This includes a combination of sensors, processors, and programming languages to enable the robot to perceive its environment, make decisions, and execute actions.

Locomotion and Control

Humanoid robots are designed to move in a way that is similar to human beings. This allows them to navigate through complex environments and interact with objects in a natural manner. To achieve this, humanoid robots use a combination of mechanical and electronic systems to control their movements. One of the key factors in humanoid locomotion is balance. Humans are able to maintain balance by constantly making small adjustments to their posture and movements. To replicate this, humanoid robots use sensors to detect their center of mass and make necessary corrections to maintain stability. Humanoid robots also use advanced control systems, such as position and torque feedback, to execute precise and complex movements. These systems allow the robot to adjust its movements based on external factors, such as changes in terrain or objects in its environment.

In recent years, there have been advancements in the development of humanoid robot control using artificial intelligence. By using machine learning algorithms, humanoid robots can adapt and improve their movements through trial and error, allowing for more fluid and natural interactions with their surroundings.

Applications of Humanoid Robots

The design and development of humanoid robots have led to numerous applications in various industries. One of the most common applications is in the field of research, where humanoid robots are used to study human movements and behaviors. By mimicking human movements, scientists can gain a better understanding of how the human body works and develop methods for improving human performance. Humanoid robots are also being used in healthcare, particularly in physical and occupational therapy. Their ability to replicate human movements makes them an effective tool for helping patients with motor impairments or injuries. They can also assist in tasks such as lifting and carrying patients, reducing the strain on healthcare workers. Another growing area for humanoid robots is in the service industry. With advancements in artificial intelligence, humanoid robots are being used in customer service roles, such as receptionists and greeters. They can also perform tasks such as cleaning and maintenance in hotels and airports. In the future, humanoid robots could play a more significant role in society, such as in elder care and education. By designing robots that resemble humans, it is believed that they can provide emotional support and companionship to elderly individuals. They can also assist in teaching and learning activities, providing a more interactive and engaging experience for students.

In conclusion, humanoid robots are the result of a collaboration between different disciplines and a testament to the advancement of technology. With their human-like appearance and abilities, they have the potential to revolutionize various industries and enhance our daily lives in ways we never thought possible. As we continue to push the boundaries of design and development, the future holds endless possibilities for humanoid robots.

Chapter 13: Robotics in Industry

Applications of Robotics in Manufacturing

Robots have been revolutionizing the manufacturing industry for decades. With their ability to perform tasks with precision, consistency, and without fatigue, robots have greatly increased efficiency and productivity in manufacturing processes. From assembly line work to material handling, robots have become an integral part of the modern manufacturing industry. One of the major applications of robotics in manufacturing is in automotive production. One of the first industries to adopt robotics in their processes, the automotive industry has seen significant improvements in speed, accuracy, and cost-effectiveness. Robots are used in tasks such as welding, painting, and assembly, where their high precision and speed greatly benefit the production process. As the demand for customized vehicles increases, robots are also being used in areas such as 3D printing, allowing for greater flexibility and adaptability in production. Another area where robotics is making a significant impact is in electronic manufacturing. As technology advances at a rapid pace, the demand for small and intricate electronic devices is also increasing. Robots are being used to handle delicate components and perform fine soldering, which would be difficult (if not impossible) for a human to do. This not only increases the speed and accuracy of the process but also reduces the risk of human error.

Industrial Automation and Control

In addition to manufacturing processes, robots are also being used for automation and control in various industries. A major advantage of using robots for automation is their ability to work non-stop without breaks, leading to increased productivity and reduced costs. This is particularly beneficial in industries such as food processing, where the production needs to be continuous. Robots are also being used in hazardous environments, such as nuclear power plants and chemical processing plants, where human presence can be dangerous. In such environments, robots are equipped with sensors and cameras, allowing them to perform tasks with precision and from a safe distance.

Another key area where robotics is being used for automation and control is in warehouse and logistics operations. With the rise of e-commerce, the demand for fast and efficient delivery has increased. Robots are being used for sorting, packaging, and loading of goods, allowing for a more streamlined and error-free process. This has resulted in faster and more accurate delivery times, leading to increased customer satisfaction.

Industry 4.0

Industry 4.0, also known as the Fourth Industrial Revolution, refers to the integration of advanced technologies such as robotics, artificial intelligence, and the Internet of Things (IoT) in manufacturing and other industries. By combining these technologies, Industry 4.0 aims to create smart factories that can communicate, analyze, and make decisions without human intervention, leading to greater efficiency and flexibility. Robots are at the forefront of Industry 4.0, with the ability to collect and analyze data, adapt to changes in the production process, and work collaboratively with humans. With the use of sensors and artificial intelligence, robots can detect and identify potential problems in the production process and adjust accordingly, leading to fewer errors and increased productivity. Furthermore, the integration of IoT in robotics allows for real-time monitoring and control of robots, leading to better decision-making and optimization of processes. This also allows for remote monitoring and control, reducing the need for human intervention in certain situations. In addition to improving efficiency and productivity, Industry 4.0 is also focused on creating a more sustainable and environmentally friendly manufacturing process. With the use of advanced technologies such as robots, energy consumption and waste production can be reduced, contributing to a more sustainable future.

In conclusion, the use of robotics in industry has brought about significant advancements in efficiency, productivity, and safety. As technology continues to evolve, we can expect to see even more sophisticated and advanced robots in the manufacturing and industrial sectors. With the integration of robotics in Industry 4.0, we are moving towards a future where smart factories will be able to operate autonomously, leading to greater efficiency, sustainability, and innovation in the industrial world.

Chapter 14: Robotic Sensors - Types, Fusion, and Networks

Introduction

In the world of robotics, sensors play a vital role in allowing robots to interact with their environment and make intelligent decisions. These sensors act as the robot's eyes and ears, providing crucial information about its surroundings. With advancements in technology, there has been significant progress in the development of sensors, making it possible for robots to have a better understanding of the world. In this chapter, we will explore the different types of sensors used in robotics, their fusion, and sensor networks.

Types of Sensors used in Robotics

Sensors used in robotics can be broadly classified into two categories: internal and external sensors. Internal sensors are those that are integrated into the robot's body and measure its internal states such as position, orientation, and velocity. External sensors, on the other hand, are used to gather information about the robot's environment. Some of the commonly used internal sensors in robotics include encoders, accelerometers, gyroscopes, and potentiometers. Encoders are used to measure the position and velocity of a robot's joints, and they are essential for tasks that require precise control and manipulation, such as robot arms. Accelerometers and gyroscopes measure the acceleration and rotation of the robot, respectively, providing information about its orientation and movement. Potentiometers are used to measure the angle or displacement of a joint, enabling precise control of the robot's movements.

External sensors, on the other hand, include cameras, lidar, ultrasound, infrared, and tactile sensors. Cameras are used for visual perception, allowing robots to recognize objects, navigate their surroundings, and even perform tasks such as object detection and tracking. Lidar, which uses lasers to measure distance and create 3D maps, is commonly used for navigation and obstacle avoidance. Ultrasound sensors emit high-frequency sound waves and use the time it takes for the sound to bounce back to calculate the distance of objects. These sensors are commonly used for precise distance measurement and obstacle detection. Infrared sensors use infrared light to detect objects and can be used for proximity and distance sensing. Tactile sensors, also known as touch sensors, can detect physical contact and pressure, allowing robots to interact with their environment and perform tasks that require gentle and delicate touch.

Sensor Data Fusion

Sensor data fusion is the process of combining data from multiple sensors to obtain a more accurate and complete understanding of the environment. It is crucial for robots to have reliable and accurate sensor data to make informed decisions and perform tasks efficiently. Sensor data fusion techniques vary depending on the type of sensors used, the environment, and the task at hand. The two main types of data fusion are sensor level and decision level. Sensor level fusion involves combining raw data from multiple sensors to produce a single, more accurate measurement of a specific variable. For example, combining data from gyroscopes and accelerometers to obtain accurate information about the robot's orientation and movements. This technique is commonly used in navigation, object tracking, and mapping applications. Decision level fusion, on the other hand, involves combining data from different sensors to make a final decision. This type of fusion is more complex and requires sophisticated algorithms to determine the reliability and relevance of each sensor's data. Decision level fusion is commonly used in tasks that require high-level decision making, such as autonomous driving and object recognition.

Sensor Networks

Sensor networks play a crucial role in modern robotics by allowing for distributed sensing and data processing. A sensor network consists of multiple sensors, either internal or external, that are connected to each other and to a central processing unit. These sensors work together to collect, process, and transmit data, allowing robots to have a more comprehensive understanding of their surroundings. One of the main advantages of sensor networks is their ability to cover a large area and provide a more detailed and accurate representation of the environment. This is especially useful in tasks such as environmental monitoring and surveillance. In addition, sensor networks can also improve the overall reliability of the robot by providing redundant data from multiple sensors.

Another significant advantage of sensor networks is their flexibility and scalability. With the advancements in wireless communication and miniaturization, sensors can now be placed in various locations, including hard-to-reach or hazardous environments. These sensors can also be easily added or removed as needed, making sensor networks highly adaptable to different applications.

Conclusion

Robotic sensors are the foundation of artificial intelligence and play a crucial role in allowing robots to interact with their environment and make intelligent decisions. With advancements in technology, sensors have become more sophisticated, providing robots with a better understanding of the world around them. By utilizing sensor fusion techniques and sensor networks, robots can perform tasks more efficiently, accurately, and safely. As technology continues to evolve, we can expect to see more advanced and versatile sensors being developed, enabling robots to perform even more complex tasks and make a significant impact in various industries.

Chapter 15: Robot Programming and Simulation

Programming Languages for Robotics

When it comes to developing and implementing software for robots, choosing the right programming language is crucial. Different programming languages offer different capabilities and strengths, and the choice ultimately depends on the specific needs of the robot and its intended tasks. In this chapter, we will explore some of the top programming languages used in robotics and their unique features.

1. C/C++
C and C++ are two of the most widely used programming languages in robotics. They offer low-level control, making them ideal for embedded systems that require fast and efficient processing. C++ is an extension of C and offers additional features such as object-oriented programming, making it easier to manage complex code. These languages are traditionally used for developing firmware for robots, as well as for high-level algorithms and tasks such as sensor data processing, control, and navigation.

2. Python
Python is a high-level, general-purpose programming language that has gained popularity in the robotics community due to its simplicity and ease of use. It offers a wide range of libraries and frameworks for artificial intelligence and machine learning, making it a popular choice for developing intelligent robots. Python's syntax is very human-readable, making it easy for researchers and hobbyists to quickly develop and test robotic applications. Some of the popular robotics frameworks that use Python include ROS (Robot Operating System) and PyRobot.

3. Java
Java is another popular programming language in the field of robotics. It offers a cross-platform environment and is widely used for developing mobile applications, making it suitable for robotics applications that require wireless communication. Java is also known for its garbage collection and memory management, making it useful for creating complex and memory-intensive robotic systems.

4. MATLAB

MATLAB is a high-level technical computing language that is widely used for scientific and engineering applications, including robotics. It offers an extensive library of built-in functions and toolboxes for various applications, such as control systems, signal processing, and image processing. This makes it a popular choice for researchers and professionals in the robotics field. Additionally, MATLAB's Simulink tool allows for graphical programming and simulation of dynamic systems, making it a valuable tool for teaching and designing robots.

Robot Simulation and Visualization

Robot simulation and visualization allows users to develop and test robotic systems in a virtual environment before deploying them in the real world. This technology has become increasingly important in the field of robotics, as it offers a more cost-effective and efficient way to design, test, and optimize robotics solutions. In this section, we will explore some of the popular software tools for robot simulation and visualization.

1. Gazebo

Gazebo is a 3D robot simulator that allows for the accurate and realistic simulation of complex robots, sensors, and environments. It offers compatibility with ROS and allows users to create and test robot models, control algorithms, and sensor simulations. Gazebo also supports physics engines such as ODE, Bullet, and Simbody, making it suitable for a wide range of applications.

2. Webots

Webots is a cross-platform simulation software that allows for the creation and simulation of robots in a virtual environment. It offers an extensive library of robot models and sensors, making it easy to create and test various robotic systems. Webots also supports advanced features such as real-time physics simulation and 3D visualization, making it a popular choice for both research and education.

3. V-REP

V-REP (Virtual Robot Experimentation Platform) is a versatile simulation software designed specifically for robotics simulation. It offers a user-friendly interface and allows for the creation of complex robots, sensor systems, and environments. V-REP offers support for a wide range of robots and platforms, making it a popular choice for industrial and academic purposes.

4. Blender

Blender is an open-source 3D modeling and animation software that offers a robust suite of tools for simulating and visualizing robotics systems. It offers physics-based simulation, real-time 3D graphics, and an intuitive interface, making it a popular choice for beginners as well as professionals.

In conclusion, choosing the right programming language and simulation tool for robotics is crucial to ensuring the success of a robotics project. It is important to consider factors such as the complexity of the robot, its intended tasks, and the available resources when making these decisions. With the advancements in technology, the capabilities and possibilities of robotics continue to expand, and it is important for engineers to stay updated on the latest trends and tools in order to design and develop innovative and efficient robots.

Chapter 16: Advanced Communication for Robotics and AI

In this chapter, we will delve into the exciting world of wireless communication, network protocols, and industrial communication standards for robotics and artificial intelligence (AI) systems. As these advanced technologies continue to revolutionize the field of electrical engineering, it is crucial to understand their capabilities, applications, and potential challenges. So, let's dive deep into this fascinating topic and explore the wonders of advanced communication in robotics and AI.

Wireless Communication

Wireless communication has been around for many decades, but its advancement in recent years has been truly remarkable. It has become a vital component of robotics and AI systems, allowing for seamless and efficient communication between devices. Gone are the days when robots had to be connected to cables and wires to function; wireless communication has set them free, making them truly autonomous. One of the most significant advancements in wireless communication for robotics and AI is the emergence of low-power wireless technologies such as Wi-Fi, Bluetooth, and ZigBee. These technologies have enabled the development of smaller, low-cost, and energy-efficient devices, making them an ideal choice for robotic and AI applications. They also provide the convenience of remote control and monitoring, making it possible for robots to work in hazardous or inaccessible environments.

Another game-changing aspect of wireless communication for robotics and AI is the emergence of 5G technology. With its ultra-fast speed and low latency, 5G has the potential to unlock new levels of connectivity and performance for robots and AI devices. It will allow for real-time processing and decision-making, making robots and AI systems more responsive, efficient, and reliable.

Network Protocols

Network protocols are essential for facilitating communication between devices and networks. In the world of robotics and AI, these protocols play a crucial role in ensuring seamless and reliable communication between various components of a system. They provide a standardized way of formatting and transmitting data, allowing devices to communicate and understand each other's commands.

Some of the most commonly used network protocols in robotics and AI are TCP/IP, MQTT, and CoAP. TCP/IP is a reliable and extensively used protocol for internet communication, making it ideal for remote monitoring and control of robots and AI systems. MQTT (Message Queuing Telemetry Transport) is a lightweight and efficient protocol designed for constrained and low-power devices, making it ideal for use in small and energy-efficient robots. CoAP (Constrained Application Protocol) is another lightweight and efficient protocol designed for use in constrained devices with limited processing power, memory, and energy.

Industrial Communication Standards

Industrial communication standards are specific protocols and interfaces designed for use in industrial settings, such as factories and manufacturing plants. They ensure the smooth integration and communication of different devices and systems, enabling efficient and effective industrial automation. In the world of robotics and AI, these standards play a pivotal role in creating smart and interconnected industrial systems.

Some of the most commonly used industrial communication standards in robotics and AI are PROFIBUS, MODBUS, and CAN bus. PROFIBUS (Process Field Bus) is a commonly used protocol for industrial automation, allowing for communication between different devices and sensors in a factory setting. MODBUS is an open-source protocol widely used for communication between control systems and devices in industrial automation. CAN bus (Controller Area Network) is a robust and highly reliable protocol designed for use in automotive and industrial applications, making it ideal for robotics and AI systems.

In conclusion, the advanced communication technologies discussed in this chapter have played a vital role in shaping the field of robotics and artificial intelligence. From wireless communication to network protocols and industrial communication standards, each of these components has contributed to the development of smarter and more efficient robots and AI systems. As these technologies continue to evolve, we can expect even more exciting advancements in the world of robotics and AI. So, let's keep exploring and pushing the boundaries of what is possible with advanced communication in robotics and AI.

Chapter 17: Artificial Neural Networks: Unleashing Potential in Robotics and AI

The field of robotics and artificial intelligence (AI) has been rapidly advancing in recent years, and one of the key technologies driving this progress is Artificial Neural Networks (ANNs). ANNs are computational models based on the structure and function of biological neural networks in the human brain. These powerful networks have the ability to learn, adapt, and make decisions, making them a valuable tool in robotics and AI applications. In this chapter, we will explore three types of ANNs – Perceptrons, Feedforward Neural Networks, and Convolutional Neural Networks – and their role in revolutionizing the field of robotics and AI.

Perceptron

The Perceptron, developed by psychologist Frank Rosenblatt in the late 1950s, is the simplest form of an artificial neural network. It consists of a single layer of artificial neurons that take in several inputs and produce a single output. The main purpose of a perceptron is to classify input data into different categories by adjusting the weights of its inputs. This process is known as supervised learning, where the network is trained on a labeled dataset and adjusts its weights until it can accurately classify new data. While the Perceptron was initially criticized for its limitations in solving complex problems, its simplicity and ability to learn have made it a fundamental component of more advanced neural networks. In robotics and AI, perceptrons are used to classify images, recognize speech, and make decisions based on data inputs, making them a crucial part of intelligent systems.

Feedforward Neural Networks

Feedforward Neural Networks (FFNNs) are the most commonly used type of ANN in the field of robotics and AI. They are composed of multiple layers of neurons that process input data and transmit it to the next layer without any feedback loops. Each neuron in a layer is connected to all the neurons in the following layer, and the weights of these connections are adjusted during the training process to improve the network's performance.

FFNNs excel in pattern recognition tasks and have been used in various robotics and AI applications, such as voice and facial recognition, natural language processing, and autonomous vehicles. They are also used in conjunction with other machine learning techniques, such as backpropagation and gradient descent, to improve their learning capabilities and accuracy.

Convolutional Neural Networks

Convolutional Neural Networks (CNNs) are a specialized type of FFNNs designed specifically for image recognition and processing. Inspired by the structure of the visual cortex in the human brain, CNNs have a series of hidden layers, each performing a different task in the image recognition process. The most crucial feature of CNNs is their ability to learn and identify features of images, such as lines, shapes, and colors, without being explicitly programmed. CNNs have revolutionized the field of computer vision, enabling robots and AI systems to accurately identify and classify objects in their environments. They have also been used in facial recognition, self-driving cars, and medical imaging, showcasing their potential in various industries and applications.

Unlocking the Potential of ANNs in Robotics and AI

Artificial Neural Networks have shown tremendous potential in robotics and AI, pushing the boundaries of what is possible in autonomous systems and intelligent machines. They have opened up new avenues for research and development, and their capabilities continue to evolve as advancements in technology are made. However, there are still challenges that need to be addressed, such as the need for massive amounts of training data, the interpretability of neural network decisions, and ensuring the ethics and safety of AI systems. As we continue to improve and innovate in the field of ANNs, we must also consider these crucial aspects to ensure a responsible and beneficial implementation of this technology.

In conclusion, Artificial Neural Networks have brought forth a new era of possibilities in robotics and AI, revolutionizing the way intelligent systems operate and learn. Their ability to learn, adapt, and make decisions based on data makes them an invaluable tool in creating autonomous, intelligent machines. As we continue to explore and develop ANNs, we can only imagine the greater potential they hold for the future of robotics and AI.

Chapter 18: Fuzzy Logic and its Applications in Robotics

Fuzzy logic is a powerful tool that has revolutionized robotics and artificial intelligence (AI). It is a mathematical approach to representing uncertainty and imprecision in reasoning, making it particularly useful in situations where traditional binary logic falls short. This chapter will delve into the fundamentals of fuzzy logic, its applications in robotics, and its potential for future advancements in the field.

Fuzzy Sets and Logic

Before delving into the intricacies of fuzzy logic, it is important to understand the basic principles of fuzzy sets. Unlike traditional sets where an element either belongs or does not belong to a set, fuzzy sets allow for degrees of membership. This is achieved by assigning a membership function to each element, which determines the degree to which the element belongs to the set. Fuzzy logic, on the other hand, is an extension of traditional binary logic that allows for values between true and false. It allows for the representation of uncertainty and partial truth, making it more suitable for real-world problems that are complex and uncertain. The foundation of fuzzy logic lies in the concept of linguistic variables and fuzzy rules. Linguistic variables allow for the representation of qualitative terms in a quantitative manner, while fuzzy rules govern the relationship between these variables. These two components work together to provide a framework for fuzzy logic systems, allowing them to handle complex decision-making processes.

Fuzzy Control

The application of fuzzy logic in control systems has been a game-changer in the field of robotics. Traditional control systems are based on precise mathematical models or algorithms, which are difficult to design and implement for complex systems. On the other hand, fuzzy control systems do not require precise mathematical models and are more suited for real-world applications. Fuzzy controllers consist of four main components: fuzzification, inference engine, rule base, and defuzzification. Fuzzification involves converting an input value into a fuzzy variable, which is then used by the inference engine to determine the appropriate fuzzy output value. The rule base contains a set of fuzzy rules that govern the overall behavior of the fuzzy controller. Finally, defuzzification converts the fuzzy output value into a crisp value that can be used to control the system.

Fuzzy control has been successfully applied in various robotics applications, including autonomous vehicles, process control, and intelligent robotic systems. One of the major advantages of fuzzy control is its ability to handle uncertainties and imprecise data, making it more robust and reliable in real-world situations. Furthermore, its ease of implementation and ability to adapt to changing environments make it a popular choice for control systems in robotics.

Applications of Fuzzy Logic in Robotics

Fuzzy logic has contributed significantly to the development of robotics, with its applications ranging from decision making to motion planning. One of the main areas where fuzzy logic has been widely used is in mobile robotics, where it plays a crucial role in navigation and mapping. The ability to handle uncertainties and partial information makes it a natural fit for robotic systems operating in dynamic and complex environments. Fuzzy logic has also found applications in robot manipulation, allowing for more human-like and flexible movements. By incorporating feedback from sensors and visual data, robots equipped with fuzzy logic can navigate and manipulate objects in a more efficient and natural manner. Moreover, fuzzy logic has been used in developing humanoid robots, allowing for more realistic and human-like interactions.

Apart from these applications, fuzzy logic has also been used in areas such as path planning, obstacle avoidance, and data fusion in robotics. Its ability to handle incomplete and uncertain data has made it a crucial tool in developing more intelligent and autonomous robots.

The Future of Fuzzy Logic in Robotics

As the field of robotics and AI continues to evolve, fuzzy logic is expected to play a more significant role in shaping the future of the industry. With advancements in sensor technology, robots equipped with fuzzy logic will be able to gather and process more data, enabling them to make more informed decisions in complex and dynamic environments. Furthermore, fuzzy logic is also gaining popularity in artificial neural networks, allowing for more efficient and accurate learning. This combination of fuzzy logic and neural networks has the potential to create more intelligent and adaptive robots that can learn and adapt to changing situations.

In conclusion, fuzzy logic has become an indispensable tool in the field of robotics and AI, allowing for more robust, efficient, and intelligent systems. From control systems to decision-making, it has shown its potential in various applications and has opened up new possibilities for future advancements. As technology continues to advance, so will the role of fuzzy logic in shaping the future of robotics.

Conclusion

In this chapter, we covered the fundamentals of fuzzy sets and logic, its applications in robotics, and its potential for future advancements. Fuzzy logic has proven to be a powerful tool, allowing for the representation of uncertainty and partial truth in solving complex problems. Its applications in control systems, navigation, and decision-making have made it an essential component in the development of more intelligent and autonomous robots. As technology continues to advance, we can expect to see more innovative applications of fuzzy logic in robotics, further pushing the boundaries of what is possible in the field.

Chapter 19: Evolutionary Robotics

The field of robotics has made tremendous strides in recent years, with machines becoming more advanced and capable than ever before. But what if we told you that machines could become even more intelligent and adaptive by mimicking the process of natural selection? This is where evolutionary robotics comes in. In this chapter, we will delve into the world of genetic algorithms, evolution strategies, and the various applications of this cutting-edge field in robotics.

Genetic Algorithms

Genetic algorithms, also known as genetic programming, is a computational evolutionary approach that aims to solve complex problems by mimicking the process of natural selection. This technique involves randomly generating a population of potential solutions and then using a fitness function to evaluate their performance. The fittest individuals are selected and bred together to produce offspring, thus creating a new population. This process is repeated over multiple generations, with the hope that the solutions will improve with each generation until an optimal solution is found.

One of the key advantages of genetic algorithms is its ability to handle high-dimensional and non-linear problems. This makes it particularly useful in the field of robotics, where complex and dynamic environments are a common challenge. With the help of genetic algorithms, robots can adapt and evolve to handle a wide range of situations, making them more versatile and efficient.

Evolution Strategies

Evolution strategies are another type of evolutionary algorithm that uses random mutations to adapt and improve solutions. This approach differs from genetic algorithms in that it does not use crossover, where individuals are mixed together to create offspring. Instead, the solutions are mutated within a population, with the most successful individuals being used to create the next generation.

One of the key advantages of evolution strategies is its ability to handle large-scale problems. This makes it particularly useful in the field of robotics, where robots must make decisions and take actions in complex and constantly changing environments. By using evolution strategies, robots can adapt and evolve their strategies to handle these challenges, ultimately leading to better performance and efficiency.

Applications of Evolutionary Robotics

The applications of evolutionary robotics are vast and diverse, with various industries and sectors benefiting from this cutting-edge technology. One such application is in the field of swarm robotics, where multiple robots work together to accomplish a task. With the help of genetic algorithms and evolution strategies, these robots can adapt and evolve their behaviors to work seamlessly together, achieving efficient and effective results. Another application of evolutionary robotics is in robot control systems. Robots must be able to navigate and manipulate their environment to perform various tasks. By using genetic algorithms and evolution strategies, these robots can adapt and optimize their control systems, leading to faster and more precise movements. Interestingly, evolutionary robotics is also being used in the design and development of robotic architectures. By incorporating genetic algorithms and evolution strategies, researchers can create and test different designs for robots, allowing for the discovery of more efficient and capable architectures.

Other industries where evolutionary robotics is gaining traction include healthcare, manufacturing, and space exploration. In healthcare, robots can be used to assist with surgeries, perform physical therapy exercises, and even provide companionship for elderly patients. In manufacturing, robots can adapt and evolve their movements to handle complex assembly tasks. And in space exploration, robots can be sent to other planets and adapt to the new environmental conditions, all thanks to the power of genetic algorithms and evolution strategies.

In Conclusion

Evolutionary robotics is an exciting and rapidly advancing field that has the potential to revolutionize the world of robotics and artificial intelligence. By mimicking the process of natural selection, machines can become more intelligent, versatile, and efficient, leading to a whole new level of technological advancement. As we continue to push the boundaries of what is possible, it is certain that evolutionary robotics will play a crucial role in shaping the future of robotics and electrical engineering.

Chapter 20: Artificial Intelligence in Robotics

As technology continues to advance at an unprecedented rate, the integration of Artificial Intelligence (AI) in robotics is becoming increasingly common. This merging of fields has allowed for the creation of more intelligent and adaptive robots, capable of performing complex tasks and even learning from their environment. In this chapter, we will explore the concept of Swarm Intelligence (SI) and its various applications in the field of robotics.

Ant Colony Optimization

Ant Colony Optimization (ACO) is a metaheuristic algorithm inspired by the behavior of ants when foraging for food. This approach involves emulating how ants communicate with each other using pheromones, which helps them to find the shortest path to a food source. In robotics, ACO has been successfully applied to path planning and task allocation problems. By employing this method, robots can efficiently navigate complex and dynamic environments, optimizing their routes while avoiding obstacles and collisions.

One of the key advantages of ACO in robotics is its ability to adapt and find optimal solutions in real-time. As ants continuously update their pheromone trails to reflect the changes in their environment, robots using ACO can also adjust their paths in response to new obstacles or changes in objectives. This enhances their efficiency and makes them more resilient to unforeseen circumstances.

Particle Swarm Optimization

Particle Swarm Optimization (PSO) is another bio-inspired metaheuristic algorithm that has gained popularity in the field of robotics. This method mimics the behavior of a flock of birds or a school of fish, where each individual follows the movement of its neighbors to find the best position in the group. In robotics, PSO has been used for path planning, motion control, and swarm coordination tasks.

One of the main benefits of PSO in robotics is its ability to handle complex and nonlinear problems. By allowing robots to communicate and learn from each other, PSO enables them to find the most efficient solutions in a timely manner. Additionally, this approach is highly scalable, making it suitable for applications involving large groups of robots working together.

Applications of Swarm Intelligence in Robotics

Swarm Intelligence has numerous applications in the field of robotics, ranging from simple tasks to more complex and challenging ones. One of the primary areas where SI has been applied is in collective decision making. Robots with swarm intelligence can autonomously make decisions based on their interactions with other robots and their observations of the environment. This allows them to work together and achieve a common goal. Another application of SI in robotics is cooperative transportation. By using swarm algorithms, robots can efficiently move and transport objects by coordinating their actions. This can be particularly useful in scenarios where a single robot may not be able to handle the load or where the environment is constantly changing.

Additionally, SI has also been used in the development of self-organizing systems, where robots can adapt and reconfigure themselves to perform a task more efficiently. This is particularly useful in situations where the environment is unpredictable, and robots need to constantly adjust to changing conditions.

Cultivating Cheerful and Cultured Artificial Intelligence

Swarm intelligence allows for the creation of more advanced and adaptive robots, but it also raises ethical concerns about the potential consequences of such developments. As we continue to integrate AI into our robotic creations, it is crucial to keep in mind the importance of cultivating a cheerful and cultured approach to their design and implementation. AI should be seen not as a replacement for human intelligence, but as a tool to enhance and support it. It is essential to consider the impact that our actions and decisions may have on society as we continue to develop and implement AI technology. By taking a cheerful and cultured approach, we can ensure that AI and robotics are used for the betterment of humanity and not to its detriment.

Conclusion

In conclusion, Swarm Intelligence has proven to be a valuable tool in the field of robotics, enabling the creation of more intelligent, adaptive, and efficient robots. By drawing inspiration from nature and utilizing advanced algorithms, SI allows for complex tasks to be performed by groups of robots working together. As we continue to explore the potential of AI in robotics, it is vital to approach its development with caution and a sense of responsibility to ensure its beneficial use for both present and future generations.

Chapter 21: Reinforcement Learning in Robotics

Robotics has greatly benefited from various branches of artificial intelligence, and reinforcement learning is one that has shown exceptional promise. Reinforcement learning is a type of machine learning that involves an agent interacting with the environment to learn how to make the best decisions. It is based on the concept of reward and punishment, where the agent learns from its past actions to make better decisions in the future. This type of learning has proved to be very effective in various applications, including robotics. In this chapter, we will explore the fundamentals of reinforcement learning and its applications in robotics.

Markov Decision Processes

Before delving into reinforcement learning, it is important to understand the concept of Markov decision processes (MDPs). MDPs are mathematical models used to describe decision-making processes in an environment. It takes into consideration the current state of the environment, possible actions, and future states. MDPs are an integral part of reinforcement learning, as it helps in calculating the expected rewards for different actions in different states. This information is crucial for the agent to make optimal decisions. In MDPs, the environment is modeled as a set of states, with each state having a set of possible actions that the agent can take. When performing an action, the environment transitions to a new state and provides the agent with a reward based on its action. This reward can be positive or negative, depending on whether the action benefits or hinders the agent's goal. The ultimate goal of the agent is to maximize its total reward over time.

Applications of Reinforcement Learning in Robotics

Reinforcement learning has many applications in the field of robotics, making it a valuable tool for engineers. One of its significant applications is in the development of autonomous robots. Autonomous robots require the ability to make decisions and adapt to their surroundings. Reinforcement learning enables them to learn from their past experiences and make better decisions in the future. Another area where reinforcement learning is useful is in motion planning and control. In tasks where precise control is necessary, traditional control methods may not be sufficient. Reinforcement learning allows the robot to explore different actions and learn which ones yield the best results. It can also adapt to changing conditions and find alternative solutions if needed. Moreover, reinforcement learning has proven to be beneficial in swarm robotics, where a group of robots work together to achieve a common goal. Each robot is considered an individual agent and uses reinforcement learning to make decisions based on its environment and interactions with other robots. This approach has shown promising results in tasks such as search and rescue missions, where coordination and cooperation among robots are vital.

In addition to these applications, reinforcement learning is also being used in the development of intelligent decision-making systems. These systems can assist humans in making complex decisions, such as in healthcare or financial planning. Reinforcement learning algorithms enable these systems to learn from data and adapt to changing conditions, making them more reliable and accurate.

In Conclusion

Reinforcement learning has become an essential tool in the development of intelligent and autonomous systems, particularly in robotics. It allows robots to learn from their environment and make informed decisions to achieve their goals. In this chapter, we explored the basics of reinforcement learning, including Markov decision processes and the Q-Learning algorithm. We also discussed some of its practical applications in robotics, highlighting its potential to revolutionize the field. As technology continues to advance, we can expect to see even more remarkable advancements in the combination of robotics and reinforcement learning.

Chapter 22: Human-Robot Interaction Ethics: Exploring the Social and Legal Implications of AI

Introduction to Human-Robot Interaction Ethics

As technology continues to advance, the field of robotics and artificial intelligence (AI) is rapidly expanding and becoming an integral part of our daily lives. From self-driving cars to virtual personal assistants, robots and AI systems are revolutionizing the way we live, work, and interact with the world. However, with this rapid growth comes the need to carefully consider the ethical implications of human-robot interaction.

In this chapter, we will dive deep into the ethics of human-robot interaction, exploring the social and legal implications of AI and discussing the importance of ethical design in robotics and AI systems.

Human-Robot Interaction Ethics

While robots have traditionally been used in factory settings, their role in society is rapidly changing as they become more advanced and integrated into our daily lives. This raises important questions about the ethics of human-robot interaction. How should we treat robots? Do they have rights? What are our responsibilities towards them? One of the key ethical considerations in human-robot interaction is the concept of moral agency. This refers to the ability to make moral decisions and be held accountable for one's actions. While humans possess this agency, robots do not. Therefore, it is important for us to carefully consider how we program and design robots to ensure that they act ethically and do not harm humans or their environment.

Social and Legal Implications of AI

As AI systems become more advanced, they are being used in a wide range of industries such as healthcare, finance, and transportation. While these advancements bring many benefits, they also raise concerns about their impact on society, particularly in terms of employment and privacy. The use of AI in the workplace has the potential to lead to a loss of jobs, especially in industries where manual labor can be replaced by machines. This raises questions about the responsibility of companies to provide job security and retraining for employees whose jobs are replaced by AI.

Furthermore, the use of AI also raises concerns about privacy. With the increasing amount of data being collected and analyzed by AI systems, there is a risk of personal information being used or accessed without consent. This highlights the need for clear regulations and guidelines to protect individuals' privacy rights.

Ethical Design of Robotics and AI Systems

As technology continues to advance, it is crucial that we design and develop robotics and AI systems with ethical considerations in mind. This means considering the potential impact of the technology on society, as well as the well-being of humans and the environment. One aspect of ethical design in robotics and AI systems is transparency. Companies and designers have a responsibility to be transparent about how their technologies work and the potential risks involved. This allows for informed decision-making and ensures that AI systems are held accountable for their actions. Moreover, ethical design also involves diversity and inclusivity. It is important for AI systems to be developed and tested by a diverse group of individuals to minimize bias and ensure that the technology benefits all members of society.

Conclusion

In conclusion, the ethical considerations of human-robot interaction are becoming increasingly important as AI and robotics continue to advance. It is crucial for us to carefully consider the social and legal implications of AI and ensure that ethical design principles are incorporated into the development of these technologies. By doing so, we can create a future where robotics and AI systems work in harmony with humanity, benefiting society and the world at large.

Chapter 23: Dynamics and Control in Robotics

PID Control

When it comes to controlling the behavior of robots, there are various techniques and algorithms that can be used. One of the most widely used and recognized methods is the PID control. PID stands for Proportional-Integral-Derivative, and it is a type of feedback control that is used to adjust the output of a system based on its error from the desired set point. In simpler terms, PID control involves continuously measuring the error between the current state of the system and the desired state, and using that information to adjust the system's behavior to reduce the error. PID control is widely used in robotics because of its simplicity, effectiveness, and adaptability. The basic concept behind PID control is to have a control loop that operates on three components: proportional, integral, and derivative. The proportional component is responsible for adjusting the system's output based on its current error. The integral component takes into account the accumulated error over time and makes adjustments accordingly. And finally, the derivative component is used to anticipate future changes and make preemptive adjustments. Together, these components work to bring the system closer to the desired state and keep it there.

PID control is an iterative process, with the system continuously measuring the error and adjusting its output. This allows the system to respond to changes in the environment or the desired state in real-time. The beauty of PID control is that it can be applied to various systems, from simple mechanical systems to complex robots. The key to its effectiveness lies in finding the right combination of the three components and fine-tuning them to match the behavior of the system.

State-Space Control

While PID control is a popular choice for controlling robots, it has its limitations. One of the main limitations is that it only takes into account the current state of the system and its error, without considering the system's dynamics and behavior. This is where state-space control comes into play. State-space control is a more advanced and sophisticated method of controlling systems, including robots. State-space control works by using a mathematical model of the system to predict its future behavior based on its current state and any external inputs. This model is represented as a set of differential equations that describe the system's dynamics. By taking into account the system's internal dynamics and its external environment, state-space control can make more accurate and efficient adjustments. In addition to being more accurate, state-space control also allows for more flexibility and adaptability. It can be used with different types of models and can handle more complex systems. This makes it an ideal choice for controlling robots, which have multiple degrees of freedom and complex behaviors.

Model Predictive Control

Lastly, we have model predictive control, which is another advanced technique used in robotics. Model predictive control (MPC) involves using a predictive model of the system to generate a control strategy that minimizes a cost function. This control strategy is then updated and recalculated at regular intervals, allowing the system to continually optimize its behavior. MPC is particularly useful in situations where there are constraints on the system's inputs or outputs. For example, in robotics, a robot arm may have limited range of movement or weight capacity. MPC can take these constraints into account and still generate an optimal control strategy to achieve the desired tasks. Another advantage of MPC is its ability to handle nonlinear systems. Most robotic systems are nonlinear, meaning their behavior cannot be explained by a simple mathematical equation. MPC can handle these types of systems and still generate effective control strategies.

In conclusion, PID control, state-space control, and model predictive control are all important tools in the world of robotics. While PID control is a popular and simple choice for controlling systems, state-space control and model predictive control offer more advanced and accurate methods to handle complex systems. As robotics continue to evolve and become more complex, advancements in control techniques will play a vital role in their development.

Chapter 24: Simulation and Modeling in Robotics

CAD for Robotics

When designing and developing robots, engineers need to have a precise understanding of the physical structure and characteristics of the robot. This is where Computer-Aided Design (CAD) comes in. CAD software allows engineers to create detailed 3D models of the robot, including its components and its movement capabilities. The use of CAD in robotics design has revolutionized the field, allowing for more accurate and efficient designs. With CAD, engineers can easily make changes and modifications to the design without having to physically build and test each iteration. This not only saves time but also reduces the cost of development. One of the key advantages of using CAD for robotics is its ability to simulate the movement and functionality of the robot. By inputting the motor parameters and other physical characteristics into the software, engineers can see how the robot will move and perform in real life. This allows for better optimization of the design and ensures that the robot will function as intended.

Virtual Prototyping

Before physical prototypes were available, engineers had to rely on drawings and calculations to design and test their robots. However, with the advent of virtual prototyping, this process has become much more efficient and accurate. Virtual prototyping involves creating a virtual model of the robot and using simulation software to test its capabilities and performance. This allows for a more thorough and detailed analysis of the robot before any physical prototyping occurs. It also allows for quicker iterations and modifications to be made, leading to a more efficient development process.

In addition, virtual prototyping reduces the risk of errors and malfunctions in the final product. By simulating the robot's behavior in different scenarios and environments, engineers can identify and address any potential issues before the physical prototype is built.

Software for Simulating and Modeling Robots

As robotics technology continues to advance, so does the software used for simulating and modeling robots. These software programs are becoming increasingly sophisticated, allowing for more detailed and accurate simulations. Some software programs even utilize Artificial Intelligence (AI) algorithms to simulate the behavior and decision-making processes of robots in various environments. This allows for a more realistic simulation, which can lead to more accurate results and predictions. In addition, many of these software programs have user-friendly interfaces, making them accessible to not only engineers but also students and hobbyists. This allows for a wider range of people to explore and learn about robotics and its capabilities. Moreover, the use of virtual reality (VR) technology in simulating and modeling robots is becoming more popular. This approach allows for a more immersive experience, giving engineers and researchers a better understanding of the robot's behavior and capabilities.

Overall, the use of software for simulating and modeling robots has greatly advanced the field of robotics. It allows for more efficient and cost-effective development of robots while also providing a deeper understanding of their functioning and capabilities.

In Conclusion

The use of CAD, virtual prototyping, and simulation software in robotics has transformed the way engineers design and develop robots. These tools not only make the process more efficient and accurate, but they also allow for better optimization and understanding of the robot's capabilities. As technology continues to advance, we can expect even more sophisticated software and tools to be developed for simulating and modeling robots. With their help, we can achieve even greater advancements in the field of robotics, leading to a brighter and more exciting future.

Chapter 25: Building Intelligent Robots

Robot Prototyping

Building an intelligent robot is no simple task. It requires a deep understanding of robotics, artificial intelligence, and electrical engineering. However, before diving into the complex world of programming and algorithms, it is important to first focus on the physical aspect of the robot - its prototype. A prototype is a preliminary version of a product, used for testing and gathering feedback. In terms of robotics, a prototype is a physical representation of the envisioned intelligent robot. This prototype not only helps in visualizing the final product, but also allows for testing and validation of the design. When it comes to prototyping, there are several important factors to consider. The first is material selection. The materials used in the prototype should be durable, lightweight, and cost effective. As the prototype is likely to undergo several modifications, it is important to use materials that are easily accessible and can be easily replaced. Another consideration is the method of fabrication. Depending on the complexity of the design, different techniques such as 3D printing, CNC machining, or handcrafting may be used. Each method has its own benefits and limitations and should be chosen based on the specific needs of the project.

The design of the prototype should also take into account the desired functionality of the final product. This may include the type of sensors and actuators required, the size and weight limitations, as well as the overall aesthetic appeal. Prototypes should also be designed with modularity in mind, allowing for easy integration of different components and any necessary future upgrades.

Testing and Validation

Once the prototype is built, the next step is to test and validate its functionality. This process involves conducting various experiments and gathering data to ensure that the prototype meets the desired specifications. One important aspect of testing a robot prototype is its ability to interact with its environment. This can include navigating through a room, picking up objects, or performing other tasks based on its programming and sensors. These tests not only help to identify any flaws in the design, but also allow for improvements to be made. Another important aspect of testing is to ensure that the prototype is able to withstand wear and tear. This is especially important for robots that may be used in harsh or unpredictable environments. Stress tests should be conducted to ensure that the prototype can withstand shocks, vibrations, and other external forces.

Once the prototype has undergone a series of tests and modifications, it is important to validate its performance against the initial design goals. This involves comparing the prototype's functionality, durability, and overall performance against the desired specifications. Any discrepancies should be addressed before moving on to the next stage.

Design Considerations

Design considerations are critical in the development of an intelligent robot. The design of the robot should not only meet its intended functionality, but also take into account safety, reliability, and user experience. One important consideration is the integration of safety measures. As robots become more intelligent and autonomous, it is crucial to ensure that they do not pose a threat to humans or their surroundings. This may involve incorporating sensors that detect and prevent collisions, programming emergency stop functions, or implementing fail-safe mechanisms. Reliability is also a key factor in robot design. The prototype should be able to consistently perform its intended tasks without frequent breakdowns or malfunctions. This not only ensures the effectiveness of the robot, but also helps to reduce maintenance and repair costs in the long run. User experience is another important consideration, especially when it comes to designing robots for commercial or consumer use. The design should be user-friendly, with intuitive controls and clear feedback to the user. This will not only improve the usability of the robot, but also enhance its overall appeal and marketability. In addition, the prototype should also be designed with scalability in mind. As technology continues to advance, the robot should be able to adapt and evolve with new components and upgrades. This not only allows for future improvements, but also extends the lifespan of the robot.

In conclusion, building an intelligent robot requires a combination of both physical and cognitive capabilities. A strong and well-designed prototype is the foundation for developing a successful and efficient robot. Through careful prototyping, testing, and validation, along with thoughtful design considerations, engineers can create intelligent robots that will revolutionize the world we live in.

Chapter 26: Machine Vision for Robotics

Machine vision, also known as computer vision, plays a crucial role in the field of robotics. It involves the use of hardware and software to allow robots to perceive and understand their environment through digital images or videos. This technology has significantly advanced in recent years, making it an integral part of robotic systems. In this chapter, we will explore the different aspects of machine vision and its application in robotics. We will delve into image processing, object detection and recognition, and depth sensing, and see how they contribute to the overall success and efficiency of robots.

Image Processing

Image processing is the manipulation and analysis of digital images to extract useful information. It is the first step in machine vision, and it involves cleaning up and enhancing images to improve their quality for further analysis. This process can include tasks such as noise removal, edge detection, and image enhancement. In robotics, image processing is essential for providing clear and accurate visual input for robots, allowing them to make intelligent decisions and perform tasks with precision. One of the most significant advantages of using image processing in robotics is that it eliminates the need for manual coding or programming of specific visual stimuli. Robots equipped with machine vision can process visual information in real-time, allowing them to adapt to changes in their surroundings efficiently. This capability makes them more versatile and adaptable, ideal for tasks that require interaction with their environment.

Object Detection and Recognition

Object detection and recognition is another critical aspect of machine vision in robotics. It involves identifying and locating objects within an image or video, determining their size, shape, and orientation. This process is crucial for robots to perceive their surroundings and understand what objects they need to interact with to complete their tasks.

With advanced algorithms and machine learning techniques, robots can now detect and recognize objects in real-time accurately. This capability has various applications in robotics, such as in self-driving cars, where the vehicle must detect and classify objects on the road to make safe and informed decisions.

Depth Sensing

Depth sensing, also known as range imaging, is the process of determining the distance between a camera and objects in its field of view. This technology is essential for robots to navigate and interact with their environment accurately. There are various methods for depth sensing, including structured light, stereo vision, and time-of-flight technology. In robotics, depth sensing is critical for tasks that require precise movement and manipulation, such as in surgical robots or manufacturing processes. It allows the robot to have a better understanding of its surroundings and make informed decisions based on the spatial information it receives.

Applications in Robotics

The use of machine vision in robotics has opened up endless possibilities for automation and efficiency in various industries. It has found applications in healthcare, agriculture, manufacturing, and even space exploration. Robots equipped with machine vision can perform intricate tasks with precision, making them ideal for tasks that require dexterity and accuracy, such as surgery or assembly line work.

In the healthcare industry, machine vision has revolutionized the field of medical robotics. It allows for more precise and non-invasive procedures, reducing the risk of human error and improving patient outcomes. In agriculture, robots with machine vision can automate tasks such as harvesting and spraying crops, increasing productivity and reducing the need for manual labor.

The Future of Machine Vision in Robotics

As technology continues to advance, we can expect even more exciting developments in the field of machine vision for robotics. With the incorporation of artificial intelligence, robots will be able to analyze and interpret visual data in more complex and dynamic environments. This capability will pave the way for robots to undertake even more challenging tasks, making them valuable assets in various industries. Another significant development is the integration of machine vision with other emerging technologies, such as virtual and augmented reality. This combination has the potential to enhance human-robot collaboration, making robots even more adaptable and efficient.

In Conclusion

Machine vision has become an essential component of robotics, allowing robots to perceive and understand their environment. With image processing, object detection and recognition, and depth sensing, robots can interact and adapt to their surroundings with accuracy and efficiency. As technology continues to evolve, we can expect even more advanced and versatile applications of machine vision in robotics, making it an exciting and promising field for electrical engineers to explore.

Chapter 27: Natural Language Processing in Robotics

Natural language processing (NLP) is an area of artificial intelligence (AI) that focuses on teaching computers to understand and analyze human language. It has become an essential component in robotics, allowing robots to communicate and interact with humans in a more natural and intuitive way. In this chapter, we will explore the different aspects of NLP and its applications in robotics.

Language Recognition

One of the main challenges in NLP for robotics is teaching robots to recognize and understand human language. This involves not only identifying words and grammar rules, but also understanding the context and nuances of language. This is a complex task, as humans often use slang, sarcasm, and idiomatic expressions, which can be difficult for robots to interpret. However, with advancements in machine learning and deep learning, robots are now able to accurately recognize and interpret human language. Natural language processing algorithms allow robots to analyze large amounts of data and learn patterns to improve their language recognition capabilities. This has made it possible for robots to understand and respond to human commands, making human-robot communication more efficient and effective.

Language Generation

Language generation is another important aspect of NLP in robotics. It refers to the ability of robots to generate language that is comprehensible to humans. This can include written text, speech, or even sign language, depending on the robot's capabilities and purpose. Language generation not only helps robots to communicate with humans, but also allows them to provide feedback, give instructions, and carry out tasks more effectively.

One of the main challenges in language generation for robots is making their language sound natural and human-like. This involves considering factors such as tone, humor, and empathy, which can greatly impact the robot's interaction with humans. To address this challenge, researchers are developing artificial intelligence algorithms that allow robots to understand the emotional content of human language and generate appropriate responses.

Natural Language Interfaces for Robots

Natural language interfaces provide a way for humans to interact with robots in a more intuitive and human-like manner. These interfaces can take various forms, such as speech recognition software, chatbots, or virtual assistants. They allow humans to communicate with robots using natural language, making it easier for people to interact with and control them. Natural language interfaces for robots have a wide range of applications, from industrial robots that can be controlled by voice commands, to virtual assistants that can help us with daily tasks. They also have the potential to assist individuals with disabilities, making it easier for them to interact with technology and perform everyday tasks.

Applications of NLP in Robotics

The use of NLP in robotics has opened up a vast array of applications in various industries. In healthcare, robots can use NLP to interact with patients and assist with their medical needs. They can also help with language translation, allowing doctors and patients to communicate effectively, regardless of language barriers. In the field of education, NLP can be used to develop intelligent tutoring systems that can interact with students in a more human-like way. These systems can engage students in natural language conversations, providing personalized learning experiences and adapting to their individual needs.

NLP is also being utilized in the development of autonomous vehicles, where it enables the vehicle to understand and respond to voice commands from the driver. This makes it easier and safer for drivers to control the vehicle, without having to take their hands off the wheel or eyes off the road.

The Future of NLP in Robotics

As technology continues to advance, the capabilities of natural language processing in robotics will only continue to grow. More sophisticated NLP algorithms and neural networks will be developed, making it possible for robots to understand and generate even more complex and nuanced language. With the integration of NLP, robots will become more human-like in their interactions and communication, allowing for more seamless collaboration between humans and machines. It will also open up new opportunities for robots to assist in various industries and make our daily lives easier and more efficient. In conclusion, natural language processing plays a vital role in enhancing human-robot interaction and communication. It enables robots to understand and generate language, making it easier for them to perform tasks and assist humans in various industries. With the continued development of NLP technology, the future of robotics looks bright, and we can expect to see even more sophisticated and intelligent robots in the years to come.

Chapter 28: Artificial Intelligence in Robotics Applications

Intelligent robots have revolutionized various industries and sectors worldwide. From manufacturing and agriculture to healthcare and hazardous environments, these intelligent machines have enhanced efficiency, speed, and accuracy in completing tasks. Robotics and artificial intelligence (AI) have co-evolved over the years, leading to the development of robots that can think, learn, and make decisions on their own. In this chapter, we will explore the various applications of AI in robotics and how it has impacted different fields.

Artificial intelligence has been integrated into robotics to create more intelligent and efficient machines. This has paved the way for the use of robotics in various fields such as medical, hazardous environments, and service industries. Let's dive deeper into how AI has revolutionized these areas through the development of intelligent robots.

Medical Robotics

Medical robotics is the use of robotic systems to assist healthcare professionals in various medical procedures. With the integration of AI, these robots can perform complex surgeries with precision, speed, and accuracy. They can also collect and analyze patient data, aiding in diagnosis and treatment planning. Intelligent surgical robots such as the Da Vinci system have enabled surgeons to perform minimally invasive surgeries with greater precision and fewer incisions, resulting in faster recovery times for patients. AI algorithms embedded in these systems assist surgeons in identifying and avoiding critical structures during surgery, minimizing the risk of complications. AI-powered robots are also being developed to assist in non-invasive medical procedures such as drug delivery, wound care, and rehabilitation. These robots can analyze patient data and adapt their movements accordingly, providing more personalized care to patients.

In addition to medical procedures, AI is also being used in healthcare facilities for administrative tasks, such as patient monitoring, scheduling appointments, and organizing patient records. This automation allows healthcare professionals to focus on patient care, leading to better treatment outcomes.

Hazardous Environment Robotics

Robots have been used in hazardous environments, such as nuclear power plants and oil rigs, to minimize the risk of human exposure to dangerous situations. With the incorporation of AI, these robots can work autonomously, making decisions and adapting to changing conditions. AI-powered robots can be equipped with sensors and cameras to detect potential hazards, reducing the risk of accidents and damage to equipment. They can also be used to perform tasks in environments that are too dangerous for humans to enter, such as inspecting pipelines or cleaning up chemical spills. These intelligent robots can also learn from their surroundings and past experiences, making them more efficient and effective in carrying out their tasks in hazardous environments.

Service Robotics

Service robotics is the use of robots in various service industries, such as hospitality, retail, and banking. With the integration of AI, these robots can interact with customers, provide recommendations, and complete transactions, resulting in a more personalized customer experience. AI-powered service robots are being used in hotels to assist with check-in and room service delivery. In retail, they can assist customers with finding products and making purchases. In banking, they can help customers with transactions and provide financial advice. These robots can also be used in customer service call centers to handle basic inquiries, freeing up human employees to focus on more complex tasks. With AI, these robots can learn from customer interactions, improving their responses and providing better customer service over time.

In addition to customer-facing roles, AI-powered robots are also being used for internal functions, such as inventory management and data entry. This automation allows businesses to be more efficient and accurate in their operations.

Conclusion

The integration of AI in robotics has transformed various industries and sectors, leading to more efficient, accurate, and personalized methods of completing tasks. Medical robotics, hazardous environment robotics, and service robotics are just a few examples of how AI has improved existing technologies and opened up new possibilities. As AI and robotics continue to co-evolve, the potential for these intelligent machines to impact and improve our way of life is endless.

Chapter 29: Intelligent Control Systems: A New Era in Robotics and AI

Intelligent Control Systems have emerged as a revolutionary approach in the field of Robotics and Artificial Intelligence. With advancements in technology and research, traditional control methods are no longer sufficient to handle the complexities of modern-day robotic systems. This has led to the development of intelligent control systems that use Artificial Intelligence (AI) techniques to enhance the performance of robots. In this chapter, we will explore the concept of Intelligent Control Systems and its role in shaping the future of robotics and AI.

Intelligent Control Systems

Intelligent Control Systems refer to the use of AI techniques in controlling and regulating the behavior of a system. These systems are designed to adapt and learn from their environment and make decisions, just like humans. Unlike traditional control methods that rely on pre-programmed instructions, intelligent control systems are capable of self-learning and self-regulating. This allows them to handle complex and dynamic environments, making them ideal for use in robotics and AI.

The development of modern intelligent control systems can be traced back to the 1970s when researchers began exploring the concept of adaptive control. As technology advanced, new AI techniques such as neural networks and fuzzy logic were introduced, leading to the development of robust intelligent control systems. Today, these systems are widely used in various industries, including manufacturing, healthcare, and transportation.

Learning Control

One of the key features of an intelligent control system is its ability to learn and adapt from its surroundings. Just like humans, these systems can observe their environment, identify patterns, and make decisions based on the data they collect. This allows them to improve their performance and make informed decisions, even in complex and unpredictable environments.

Learning control techniques, such as reinforcement learning and deep learning, are critical in the development of intelligent control systems. These techniques enable the system to gather information, analyze it, and use it to improve its performance. This not only makes the system more efficient but also reduces the need for human intervention, making it ideal for use in autonomous robots.

Robust Control Methods

Robustness is a crucial factor in the successful implementation of intelligent control systems in robotics and AI. Robust control methods aim to ensure that the system can operate efficiently and handle any unforeseen disturbances or uncertainties in the environment. This is essential in making the system reliable and safe to use in real-world applications. Various robust control methods, such as H-infinity control and sliding mode control, have been developed to address the challenges faced by traditional control techniques, such as sensitivity to disturbances. These methods use AI techniques, such as neural networks and fuzzy logic, to handle uncertainties and make the system more robust and stable.

The Future of Intelligent Control Systems in Robotics and AI

The use of intelligent control systems in robotics and AI has opened up new possibilities and opportunities. With the development of advanced AI techniques, we can expect these systems to become even more capable and efficient in the coming years. This will lead to the emergence of advanced autonomous robots that can handle complex tasks and adapt to their environment in real-time.

Intelligent control systems also have the potential to revolutionize various industries, such as healthcare and transportation. These systems can be used to develop advanced medical robots that can assist in surgeries and diagnosis, as well as autonomous vehicles that can navigate through traffic and make decisions in real-time.

Conclusion

Intelligent control systems have brought a new era in the field of robotics and AI. With their ability to learn and adapt, these systems are proving to be a game-changer in various industries. As technology continues to advance, we can expect intelligent control systems to become even more sophisticated and capable, shaping the future of robotics and AI.

Chapter 30: Building Beneficial and Ethical AI Systems

Artificial Intelligence (AI) has quickly become a buzzword in the field of electrical engineering, promising endless possibilities and potential. From self-driving cars to intelligent personal assistants, AI has become an integral part of our daily lives. However, with great power comes great responsibility, and as engineers, it is our duty to design AI systems that not only benefit society but also adhere to ethical standards. In this chapter, we will delve into the crucial aspects of building beneficial and ethical AI systems.

Beneficial AI Design

When it comes to developing AI systems, the focus is often on making them smarter and more capable. However, it is equally important to ensure that these systems have a positive impact on society. The concept of beneficial AI design is centered around creating systems that not only fulfill their intended purpose but also do so in a way that benefits humanity. Here are some key considerations to keep in mind when designing beneficial AI systems.

1. Human-Centered Design

The first step towards building beneficial AI is to adopt a human-centered approach. This means understanding the needs and values of the end-users and designing the system accordingly. Engineers must work closely with experts from different fields, including sociologists, psychologists, and ethicists, to ensure that the AI system aligns with the values and needs of society.

2. Transparency and Explainability

One of the biggest concerns with AI systems is the lack of transparency and explainability. As engineers, it is our responsibility to design systems that are transparent and explainable. This means making the decision-making process of the AI system understandable to humans. By doing so, we can build trust and accountability in AI systems.

3. Bias-Free Design

AI systems are only as unbiased as the data they are trained on. Unfortunately, data bias is a prevalent issue in the development of AI systems. Engineers must take the necessary measures to identify and eliminate any biases in the data to ensure fair and equal treatment for all individuals.

Ethical Considerations in AI Design

As engineers, we have a moral responsibility to ensure that the technology we create is used for the betterment of society. This means taking into account ethical considerations when designing AI systems. Here are some key ethical considerations to keep in mind when developing AI systems.

1. Privacy and Security

With the rapid advancement of AI technology, the risk of data privacy and security breaches also increases. Engineers must ensure that the AI system is designed with robust security measures in place to protect the privacy of users' data.

2. Accountability and Responsibility

As the creators of AI systems, engineers must take responsibility for the actions of their creations. This means designing systems that are accountable and have mechanisms in place to rectify any potential harm caused by the system.

3. Human Oversight

While AI systems are capable of performing complex tasks, they are still machines and can make errors. Engineers must design systems that allow for human oversight and intervention to ensure that the system does not cause any unintended harm.

Conclusion

In conclusion, as engineers, we have a responsibility to build AI systems that not only benefit society but also adhere to ethical standards. This involves adopting a human-centered design approach, ensuring transparency and explainability, eliminating biases, and taking into account ethical considerations such as privacy, accountability, and human oversight. By following these principles, we can create AI systems that not only enhance our daily lives but also contribute to a better and more ethical world.

Chapter 31: Building Intelligent Robots

Cognitive Robotics

In the world of robotics, the concept of cognitive robotics is an area of study that aims to equip robots with cognitive properties that allow them to think, reason, and make decisions like humans do. This emerging field of research involves the integration of various disciplines such as robotics, artificial intelligence, and cognitive science in order to create intelligent robots that can interact with their environment in a meaningful and autonomous way. One of the key components of cognitive robotics is the ability for robots to perceive and interpret their surroundings. This involves harnessing a combination of sensors and perception algorithms that allow robots to gather information from their environment and make sense of it. With sophisticated sensor systems, robots can perceive objects, obstacles, and even human actions, and use this information to make decisions and perform tasks.

With the integration of cognitive abilities, robots are able to understand and adapt to changing situations, making them more versatile and efficient in completing tasks. This is especially important in situations where robots are required to work alongside humans, as their cognitive abilities allow them to respond to and collaborate with human actions and movements.

Cognitive Architectures

In order for robots to possess cognitive abilities, they need a robust and efficient cognitive architecture that allows them to process information, learn from their environment, and make decisions. The most widely used cognitive architectures in robotics are based on artificial neural networks, which mimic the processes of human cognition. These architectures enable robots to learn and adapt to new situations, as well as perform complex tasks by breaking them down into smaller, more manageable steps. They also allow robots to recognize patterns and make predictions, making them intelligent and aware of their environment.

Integration of Sensors

Sensors play a crucial role in the cognitive abilities of robots. They provide robots with the necessary data to understand and interact with their environment, making them more aware and responsive. The development of advanced sensor technologies has greatly enhanced the capabilities of robots in terms of perception and cognition.

One example is the use of vision sensors, such as cameras and 3D scanners, which enable robots to see and interpret their surroundings. With these sensors, robots can recognize objects, detect human emotions and gestures, and build maps of their surroundings, allowing them to navigate and interact with their environment more effectively.

Perception in Intelligent Robots

Perception is the process by which robots gather information about their environment through sensors and interpret it to make decisions. In intelligent robots, perception is a complex and multifaceted process, involving the integration of different types of sensors and perception algorithms. By integrating perception with cognitive abilities, robots can understand and respond to their environment in a more human-like manner. For example, a robot with advanced perception capabilities can recognize emotions in humans and adjust its behavior accordingly, making it more socially intelligent. The integration of perception and cognition in intelligent robots is crucial in the development of machines that can function autonomously and interact with humans in various settings. It allows for more natural and seamless interactions between humans and robots, opening up possibilities for their use in various industries such as healthcare, manufacturing, and entertainment.

In conclusion, the field of cognitive robotics is continuously evolving and pushing the boundaries of what robots can do. Through the integration of cognitive abilities, advanced sensor technologies, and perception algorithms, intelligent robots are becoming more human-like in their interactions and abilities. As we continue to explore and develop this field, the possibilities for the use of intelligent robots will only continue to expand, shaping the future of robotics and artificial intelligence.

Chapter 32: Intelligent Decision Making in Robotics

Decision making is an essential aspect of any intelligent system, and robotics and artificial intelligence (AI) are no exception. In the field of robotics, decision making under uncertainty is a critical skill that enables robots to operate in complex and dynamic environments. It involves selecting the most optimal action based on the available information and dealing with uncertainties and factors such as noise, incomplete data, and changing conditions.

Decision Making Under Uncertainty

Uncertainty is an inevitable factor in real-world applications, and for intelligent robots, it is a constant challenge. The ability to make decisions under uncertainty is what separates advanced robots from basic ones. The uncertainty may arise from various sources, such as perception errors, environmental changes, and unpredictable events. However, an intelligent robot should have the capability to deal with these uncertainties and make optimal decisions.

In decision making under uncertainty, there are two main types of approaches: reactive and deliberative. Reactive approaches focus on navigating through the environment and responding to changes in real-time. On the other hand, deliberative approaches involve using a predefined model and reasoning to make decisions. A combination of these two approaches is often used in intelligent robots to achieve a balance between agility and accuracy.

Planning Algorithms

Planning is a critical component of intelligent decision making in robotics. It involves generating a sequence of actions to achieve a predefined goal or task. Planning algorithms are used to determine the optimal sequence of actions for each situation, considering various constraints and uncertainties. These algorithms also take into account the capabilities and limitations of the robot to ensure the plan is executable.

There are several planning algorithms used in robotics, such as A*, D*, and RRT (Rapidly-exploring Random Tree). These algorithms use different approaches to generate a suitable plan based on the robot's environment and goals. Some algorithms use heuristics to guide the search process, while others use probabilistic models to account for uncertainties. The choice of planning algorithm depends on the specific application and the type of environment the robot will operate in.

Optimal Decision Making

Optimal decision making is a crucial aspect of intelligent robots, as it allows them to perform tasks more efficiently and effectively. It involves selecting the best course of action from a set of possible options, considering various factors such as time, cost, and risks. Optimal decision making also involves evaluating the available options and choosing the one that will lead to the desired outcome with the highest probability. To achieve optimal decision making, intelligent robots use a combination of techniques such as decision-making algorithms, probabilistic models, and machine learning. For instance, reinforcement learning is often used to train robots to make optimal decisions in specific tasks by rewarding them for taking the correct actions. This deep learning approach enables robots to continuously improve their decision-making abilities based on trial and error.

In conclusion, decision making under uncertainty, planning algorithms, and optimal decision making are vital components of intelligent decision making in robotics. These skills allow robots to navigate complex and uncertain environments, plan and execute their actions effectively, and make optimal decisions to achieve their goals. As researchers continue to advance in these areas, we can expect to see even more sophisticated and intelligent robots in the future that can handle complex tasks and scenarios with ease.

Chapter 33: Human-Computer Interaction with AI and Robotics

Natural User Interfaces

The evolution of human-computer interaction has come a long way since the days of bulky keyboards and confusing command lines. With the advancement of artificial intelligence and robotics, user interfaces have become more intuitive and natural for users. Natural user interfaces (NUIs) are a type of user interface that allows users to interact with computers and other devices in a more natural and seamless manner, without the need for a traditional input device such as a mouse or keyboard. NUIs utilize gestures, voice recognition, and other advanced technologies to create an effortless and enjoyable user experience.

One example of a natural user interface is the Microsoft Kinect, which allows users to control their devices through body movements and gestures. This technology has been used not only in gaming but also in healthcare, education, and even retail industries. NUIs have also revolutionized the way we interact with our smartphones, with features such as voice commands and facial recognition becoming standard.

Gesture and Voice Recognition

Gesture and voice recognition are at the forefront of natural user interfaces. These technologies allow users to interact with devices through hand movements and spoken commands, making the traditional mouse and keyboard seem obsolete. With the use of cameras, sensors and sophisticated algorithms, gesture and voice recognition can accurately interpret user actions and commands.

One major area where gesture recognition has made a significant impact is in healthcare. Surgeons can control medical equipment hands-free, allowing for a more sterile environment and improved precision. Voice recognition, on the other hand, has been implemented in various smart home devices, making it easier for users to control their home appliances and gadgets. With the increasing demand for more efficient, hands-free interfaces, the development of gesture and voice recognition technologies will continue to grow.

Human-Centered Design

As technology becomes more integrated into our daily lives, it is essential to consider human-centered design when developing user interfaces. Human-centered design is an approach that focuses on creating user interfaces that are intuitive, efficient, and enjoyable for users. It involves understanding the needs and behaviors of users and designing interfaces that cater to these factors. One example of human-centered design in action is the use of chatbots in customer service. These artificial intelligence-powered assistants are designed to understand and respond to human interactions, making the customer experience more personalized and efficient. Human-centered design also takes into consideration the accessibility of interfaces for individuals with disabilities, ensuring that technology is inclusive for all.

In the world of robotics, human-centered design plays a crucial role in creating user-friendly and efficient robots. Designers must consider the physical and cognitive abilities of users when developing robots to perform tasks in different environments. With the advancement of artificial intelligence and machine learning, robots can adapt and learn from human interactions, leading to more natural and effortless user experiences.

In Conclusion

Human-computer interaction with AI and robotics has come a long way, and the development of natural user interfaces, gesture and voice recognition, and human-centered design have played a significant role in this progress. These technologies have not only made our interactions with devices more seamless and effortless but also have opened up a whole new world of possibilities in various industries. As technology continues to advance, the development of more intuitive and human-centric interfaces will undoubtedly shape our interactions with devices in the future.

Chapter 34: Artificial Intelligence and Robotics – Exploring the Power of Neural Networks and Reinforcement Learning

In our ever-evolving technological landscape, Artificial Intelligence (AI) and Robotics have become some of the most exciting and groundbreaking fields. With the help of advanced algorithms and intelligent systems, robots are now able to perform complex tasks and learn from their environment just like humans. This incredible progress is largely attributed to the use of neural networks and reinforcement learning techniques. In this chapter, we will delve deeper into these powerful tools and explore how they are transforming the realm of robotics and AI.

Convolutional Neural Networks

Convolutional Neural Networks (CNNs) are a type of artificial neural network that specializes in image and video analysis, specifically in computer vision tasks. They are inspired by the visual cortex of the human brain and are designed to extract spatial features from images by convolving a series of learned filters with the input data. This allows them to effectively recognize patterns and objects within images with high accuracy. One of the most significant breakthroughs in computer vision can be attributed to CNNs, specifically in image recognition tasks. Today, CNNs are used in a wide range of applications, from self-driving cars to facial recognition technology, and they continue to push the boundaries of AI and robotics.

Recurrent Neural Networks

Recurrent Neural Networks (RNNs) are another type of artificial neural network that is designed to process sequential data such as text, speech, and time series data. What sets RNNs apart from traditional neural networks is their ability to retain information over time, making them ideal for tasks that involve temporal dynamics.

The development of RNNs has opened up a whole new realm of possibilities for AI and robotics. They have shown remarkable results in language translation, speech recognition, and natural language processing. In the field of robotics, RNNs are being used to improve robot navigation and interaction with the environment, allowing for more fluid and intuitive movements.

Deep Reinforcement Learning

Reinforcement learning is a subset of machine learning, where an agent learns to interact with an environment by receiving rewards or punishments for its actions. Deep Reinforcement Learning (DRL) takes this concept to the next level by combining reinforcement learning with deep learning techniques.

DRL has proven to be a game-changer in the field of robotics. By enabling agents to learn from their environment and make decisions based on data, instead of pre-programmed instructions, they can adapt to changing situations and tasks. This has allowed robots to perform complex tasks such as grasping and object manipulation with dexterity and accuracy.

The Power of Neural Networks and Reinforcement Learning in Robotics

The progress we have witnessed in robotics and AI over the past few decades would not have been possible without the advancements in neural networks and reinforcement learning. These techniques have given robots the ability to perceive, reason, and learn from their environment, bringing them one step closer to human-like intelligence. One of the most significant advantages of using neural networks and reinforcement learning in robotics is their flexibility and adaptability. Traditional robots are restricted to performing pre-programmed tasks, making them inflexible and unable to react to unexpected situations. With neural networks, robots can learn from experience and adapt to new situations, making them more versatile and useful in real-world scenarios.

Moreover, neural networks and reinforcement learning have allowed robots to perform complex tasks with accuracy and efficiency. From recognizing objects and understanding language to navigating complex environments and making decisions, robots are now able to handle a wide range of tasks that were previously impossible.

A Bright Future Ahead

With the continuous advancements in neural networks and reinforcement learning, the future of AI and robotics looks incredibly promising. As technology continues to evolve, we can expect to see even more applications of these techniques in various industries, from healthcare and agriculture to energy and transportation. There are still challenges to overcome, such as ensuring ethical use of AI and addressing concerns about job displacement. However, with responsible use and continued research and development, we can harness the full potential of neural networks and reinforcement learning to create a better, more efficient, and intelligent future.

In conclusion, we are at a remarkable point in history where we have the technology and tools to create intelligent and autonomous robots. Neural networks and reinforcement learning have paved the way for this progress, and with their continued use and advancement, we are set to witness even more remarkable feats in the field of robotics and AI.

Chapter 35: Building Intelligent Robots for Autonomous Driving

Vision Systems for Autonomous Driving

Autonomous driving has been a dream for many decades, and with the advancements in technology and Artificial Intelligence, it is now becoming a reality. One of the key components of autonomous driving is the vision system, which allows the vehicle to "see" its surroundings and make real-time decisions. This system includes cameras, LiDAR, radar, and other sensors that collect data from the environment and provide crucial information to the vehicle's AI system. One of the biggest challenges in developing vision systems for autonomous driving is the ability to accurately identify and recognize objects in real-time. Traditional computer vision algorithms struggle with this task as they require extensive training and precise specifications for each object. However, with the use of deep learning and Convolutional Neural Networks (CNNs), vehicles can now identify objects with a high level of accuracy, making autonomous driving much safer and efficient.

Another important aspect of vision systems for autonomous driving is the ability to process vast amounts of data in real-time. With the increased number of sensors in autonomous vehicles, the systems need to quickly analyze and interpret the data to make timely decisions. This is where advancements in graphics processing units (GPUs) and parallel computing have played a significant role in enabling real-time vision processing for autonomous vehicles.

Sensor Fusion

One sensor alone is not enough to provide a complete understanding of the vehicle's surroundings. This is where sensor fusion comes into play. Sensor fusion is the process of combining data from multiple sensors to create a more precise understanding of the environment. For autonomous vehicles, this is a critical step in ensuring the safety of passengers and other road users. Sensor fusion combines data from cameras, LiDAR, radar, and other sensors to create a complete 3D representation of the surrounding area. This allows the vehicle to identify and track objects, predict their movements, and make informed decisions in real-time. The use of multiple sensors also adds redundancy, ensuring that the vehicle has alternative data sources in case of sensor failure.

However, sensor fusion is not just about combining data. It also involves complex algorithms that use machine learning and AI to interpret and make sense of the data. This is where the role of electrical engineers becomes crucial in developing sophisticated and reliable sensor fusion systems for autonomous vehicles.

Machine Learning in Autonomous Vehicles

Machine learning has revolutionized the development of autonomous vehicles. Unlike traditional software development, where programmers manually code rules and algorithms, machine learning allows the vehicles to learn and adapt based on data. This has significantly improved the accuracy and efficiency of autonomous vehicles. One of the most important applications of machine learning in autonomous vehicles is in decision making. With the use of reinforcement learning, the vehicle can analyze data from its environment and learn how to make decisions based on a set of predefined goals. This allows the vehicle to navigate through challenging situations, such as unanticipated obstacles or road closures, with minimal human intervention.

Machine learning also plays a crucial role in the optimization of various systems in autonomous vehicles. For example, it can be used to optimize the vehicle's energy consumption, route planning, and even sensor fusion algorithms. This not only improves the performance of the vehicle but also reduces its environmental impact.

Challenges and Future of Autonomous Driving

While the advancements in vision systems, sensor fusion, and machine learning have made autonomous driving a reality, there are still challenges that need to be addressed. One of the biggest challenges is achieving full autonomy, where a vehicle can navigate any road and weather condition without any human intervention. This requires extensive testing and improvement of the AI systems to ensure they can handle any situation. Another challenge is the integration of autonomous vehicles into existing transportation systems. This not only involves technical challenges but also legal and societal implications that need to be addressed. It is crucial for all stakeholders to work together to create a safe and efficient environment for autonomous vehicles to operate. The future of autonomous driving is exciting and promising. With continued advancements in technology and the collaboration of engineers from various fields, we can expect to see fully autonomous vehicles on our roads in the near future. This will not only revolutionize the way we travel but also have a significant impact on our society and the environment.

In conclusion, the development of vision systems, sensor fusion, and machine learning has been crucial in making autonomous driving a reality. The role of electrical engineers in this field is vital, and with their continued efforts and innovation, we can expect to see further advancements in this area. We must also consider the ethical implications of autonomous driving and work towards creating a safe and responsible future for this technology. The future of transportation is autonomous, and we must embrace it with caution and enthusiasm.

Chapter 36: Precision Agriculture and the Role of Robotics and AI

Precision agriculture is an innovative and dynamic approach to farming that utilizes advanced technological tools to optimize farm operations. With the use of robotics and artificial intelligence (AI), precision agriculture has transformed from traditional farming methods to more precise, efficient and sustainable techniques. This chapter will delve into the exciting world of precision agriculture, its significance in the agricultural sector, and the groundbreaking use of robotics and AI in this field.

Precision Agriculture

Precision agriculture is a modern farming management concept that involves the use of advanced technology to monitor, analyze and optimize agricultural operations. This method allows farmers to obtain valuable data about their crops, soil, and environmental conditions through the use of sensors, drones, and satellite imagery. This data is then processed and analyzed using AI algorithms, providing farmers with valuable insights to make informed decisions about their farming practices.

Autonomous Farming

One of the key elements of precision agriculture is autonomous farming, which refers to the use of robotics and AI to perform tasks without human intervention. Autonomous farm equipment, such as tractors, seeders, and crop sprayers are equipped with advanced sensors and navigation systems that allow them to operate efficiently and precisely. These autonomous devices can analyze data in real-time and adjust their movements accordingly, resulting in improved accuracy and reduced human error.

Automated Harvesting

One of the most challenging and labor-intensive tasks in agriculture is harvesting. With advancements in robotics and AI, there has been a significant shift towards automated harvesting in recent years. Automated harvesters have the ability to identify and differentiate between ripe and unripe crops, allowing for a more efficient and timely harvest. These machines can also work 24/7, ensuring that crops are harvested at the optimal time, resulting in increased yield and reduced waste.

Precision Agriculture and Sustainable Farming

The introduction of precision agriculture has brought about a paradigm shift in farming practices, moving towards a more sustainable and environmentally friendly approach. With the use of sensors, AI, and drones, farmers can collect data on soil moisture, temperature, and nutrient levels, allowing for precise and targeted use of resources such as water and fertilizers. This leads to reduced water and chemical usage, minimizing the impact on the environment and promoting sustainable farming methods.

The Role of Robotics and AI in Precision Agriculture

The use of robotics and AI has revolutionized precision agriculture by providing farmers with a wealth of data and analysis to make more informed decisions. These technologies have the ability to process large amounts of data in real-time, providing farmers with valuable insights to optimize their farming practices. Whether it is identifying and treating pests and diseases, or predicting crop yields, robotics and AI are fundamental in improving the efficiency and sustainability of precision agriculture.

Challenges and Opportunities

Despite the numerous benefits of precision agriculture, there are still challenges that need to be addressed. Some of the challenges include the high initial cost of implementing these technologies, lack of skilled labor to operate them, and data management and security issues. However, the potential for precision agriculture to increase productivity, reduce waste, and promote sustainable farming practices is immense.

The Future of Precision Agriculture and Robotics

As technology continues to advance, the future of precision agriculture and the use of robotics and AI in farming holds great promise. From autonomous drones and robots to advanced data analytics, the potential for these technologies to transform the agricultural sector is limitless. With the increasing demand for food production to feed a growing population, precision agriculture will play a crucial role in meeting these demands sustainably and efficiently.

In conclusion, precision agriculture and the use of robotics and AI have paved the way for a more efficient, sustainable, and productive farming industry. From autonomous farming equipment to data-driven decision making, these advancements have the potential to revolutionize the agricultural sector. As we continue to face challenges in food production, precision agriculture and the use of robotics and AI will be essential in ensuring food security and promoting sustainable farming practices.

Chapter 37: Robotics in Healthcare

Medical Robotics

When we think of robots, we often picture machines in factories or futuristic science fiction movies. However, robots are making their way into the healthcare industry, changing the way we approach medical treatments and procedures. Medical robotics combines the precision and efficiency of machines with the expertise and care of medical professionals to provide better patient outcomes. The use of robots in surgery has revolutionized the medical field. With the help of robots, surgeries can be performed with greater precision and accuracy, reducing the risk of human error. This is especially beneficial in delicate or complex procedures, where even the smallest mistake can have severe consequences. Robotic surgery also allows for minimally invasive procedures, with smaller incisions and less trauma to the patient's body. This results in shorter recovery times, less pain, and less scarring. Furthermore, medical robotics can be used in procedures that were previously impossible for humans to perform manually, expanding the possibilities for treatment options. One example of medical robotics is the da Vinci surgical system, a multi-arm robotic system that enables surgeons to operate through a few small incisions. This system provides 3D HD visualization, enhanced dexterity, and tremor reduction, making surgical procedures less invasive and more precise. Telemedicine is another area where medical robotics has a significant impact. With the help of telepresence robots, doctors can remotely examine and diagnose patients, reducing the need for in-person consultations. These robots have mounted cameras, microphones, and screens, allowing doctors to communicate with patients and access medical records from a remote location.

The use of medical robotics in telemedicine is particularly helpful in rural or underprivileged areas, where access to medical professionals is limited. It also provides a way for patients in isolated or quarantined situations to receive medical care without risking the spread of infectious diseases.

Telemedicine

Telepresence robots are not just limited to medical professionals. They can also be used for virtual check-ins with patients, allowing doctors to monitor their progress and make necessary adjustments to their treatment plans. These robots can also assist healthcare providers with routine check-ups, medication management, and mental health support. In emergency situations, telemedicine robots equipped with medical supplies can be deployed to the scene, providing immediate medical attention to patients before they can be transported to a hospital. This can be life-saving in critical situations, where every minute counts.

The use of telemedicine and medical robotics also addresses the growing issue of physician shortages. As the population ages and the demand for healthcare increases, there is a growing need for more healthcare professionals. By utilizing telemedicine, doctors can extend their reach and treat more patients without the need for additional physical resources.

Assistive Robotics

Aside from surgeries and telemedicine, medical robotics also plays a significant role in assisting individuals with physical disabilities. These assistive robots can provide support with daily tasks like getting in and out of bed, dressing, and eating. They can also provide rehabilitation services by guiding patients through exercises and movements to improve their motor skills. With the help of artificial intelligence, assistive robots can learn and adapt to a person's movements and preferences, making them more efficient and personalized. This reduces the need for constant human supervision, allowing individuals with disabilities to have more independence and control over their lives. Assistive robotics also provides relief for caregivers, who often bear the physical and emotional burden of taking care of a loved one with a disability. These robots can assist with lifting and transferring patients, reducing the risk of caregiver injuries and burnout.

In addition to physical disabilities, medical robotics can also assist individuals with cognitive impairments. Robots equipped with speech recognition and natural language processing technology can act as personal assistants, reminding patients to take their medication, schedule appointments, and perform daily tasks.

The Future of Healthcare and Robotics

The use of medical robotics is continuously evolving and expanding, paving the way for better healthcare and patient outcomes. As technology advances, we can expect to see further integration of robotics in medical procedures and treatments. This will not only improve the quality of healthcare but also make it more accessible for those who may not have had access to it before. Ethical considerations also come into play with the use of medical robotics. As robots become more advanced and take on more responsibilities, it is crucial to address concerns related to safety, privacy, and patient autonomy. Proper regulations and guidelines must be put in place to ensure the ethical use of medical robotics in the healthcare industry.

In conclusion, the use of robotics in healthcare is a game-changer for the industry. From improving surgical procedures to providing remote care and assisting individuals with disabilities, medical robotics has the potential to transform the way we approach healthcare and improve the lives of patients and caregivers. With continued research and development, the future of healthcare and robotics is full of promise and potential.

Chapter 38: Artificial Intelligence in Energy Systems

The world's demand for energy is constantly increasing, and with it, the need for more efficient and sustainable energy systems. As electrical engineers, it is our responsibility to find innovative ways to meet this demand while also reducing our carbon footprint. This is where artificial intelligence (AI) comes into play – it has the potential to revolutionize the energy industry and drive us towards a greener, smarter future.

Smart Grids

Smart grids are electrical grids equipped with advanced sensors, controls, and communication technologies. With the integration of AI, smart grids can become even more efficient by dynamically adapting to changing energy demands and optimizing energy distribution. AI algorithms can analyze huge amounts of data from various sources to predict energy demand and adjust supply accordingly, reducing waste and improving overall grid performance. One example of AI in smart grids is demand response – a system that incentivizes consumers to reduce their energy usage during peak hours. AI algorithms can analyze consumer behavior and patterns to accurately predict when energy demand will be high, and send signals to appliances equipped with smart technology to adjust their energy consumption accordingly. This results in reduced strain on the grid during peak hours and rewards for consumers who participate in the program.

Demand Response

As mentioned, demand response is a key aspect of smart grids and AI in energy systems. By reducing energy usage during peak hours, we can avoid blackouts and reduce the need for costly and environmentally harmful energy generators. It also encourages consumers to be more conscious about their energy usage and rewards them for making sustainable choices.

In addition to peak load management, AI is also being used in demand response to predict individual energy usage patterns for homes and businesses. This allows for more accurate forecasting and enables utilities to provide customized energy plans for their customers. For example, a household with a higher demand for energy during certain hours may receive a different plan than a household that primarily uses energy during off-peak hours.

Renewable Energy Prediction

Renewable energy sources, such as solar and wind power, have the potential to reduce our reliance on fossil fuels and decrease carbon emissions. However, their intermittent nature makes it challenging to predict energy output and integrate them into the grid effectively. This is where AI comes in – it can analyze historical data, weather patterns, and other variables to accurately predict renewable energy output. With this information, AI algorithms can optimize energy storage and distribution to ensure a consistent and reliable supply of renewable energy. This is crucial in maximizing the benefits of clean energy and minimizing the use of traditional energy sources.

Benefits of AI in Energy Systems

The integration of AI in energy systems offers numerous benefits. Firstly, it can improve the efficiency and reliability of the grid by optimizing energy production, distribution, and consumption. This results in cost savings for both utilities and consumers. Secondly, AI can help reduce our carbon footprint by promoting the use of renewable energy and optimizing energy usage. This aligns with global efforts to combat climate change and transition towards more sustainable energy sources.

Lastly, AI also has the potential to enhance grid security. With advanced monitoring and predictive capabilities, AI algorithms can detect and respond to potential security threats, keeping the grid and the energy supply safe for consumers.

Future of AI in Energy Systems

As AI technology continues to advance, its potential in energy systems is limitless. We can expect to see more integration of AI in smart grids, demand response programs, and renewable energy prediction. Additionally, AI could also be used for energy forecasting, asset management, and energy trading.

Moreover, the development of autonomous technologies, such as electric and self-driving vehicles, will also rely heavily on AI in energy systems. This will require a more interconnected grid, with AI playing a crucial role in monitoring and managing the energy needs of these technologies.

Conclusion

In conclusion, AI has the potential to transform our energy systems and drive us towards a greener, more sustainable future. It offers numerous benefits, including improved grid efficiency, reduced carbon footprint, and enhanced security. As we continue to develop and integrate AI technologies, we can expect to see significant advancements in the energy industry and move closer to our goal of a cleaner, smarter world. As electrical engineers, it is our responsibility to embrace these advancements and harness the power of AI to create a better world for future generations.

Chapter 39: Challenges and Opportunities in Robotics and AI

Technological Advancements

The field of Robotics and Artificial Intelligence has experienced remarkable growth and advancements in recent years. Through continuous research and development, engineers have been able to create robots and AI systems that were once deemed impossible. These technological advancements have not only revolutionized industries such as manufacturing and healthcare, but also our daily lives. From automated cars to virtual assistants, technology has become an integral part of our society. One of the most significant advancements in robotics and AI is the integration of Machine Learning and Deep Learning. These technologies have allowed robots and AI systems to learn and improve their performance without being explicitly programmed. This has opened up endless possibilities and applications for these technologies, making them more efficient and adaptable. With the rapid growth of the Internet of Things (IoT), robots and AI systems can now communicate and collect data in real-time, making them even more powerful and intelligent.

Another technological advancement that has contributed to the growth of robotics and AI is the development of sophisticated sensors and actuators. These components allow robots to sense and interact with their environment, making them more autonomous and versatile. Additionally, advancements in computer vision have enabled robots to see and recognize objects, enabling them to perform tasks that were previously only possible for humans.

Ethical Considerations

While the technological advancements in robotics and AI have brought many benefits, they have also raised ethical concerns. With the increasing autonomy of robots and AI systems, there are concerns about the potential loss of jobs and the impact on the economy. There is also the ethical consideration of the use of these technologies in military applications, raising questions about the development and use of autonomous weapons.

Furthermore, as robots and AI become more integrated into our daily lives, there are concerns about data privacy, security, and bias. AI systems can only make decisions based on the data they are trained on, which can lead to biased outcomes. It is essential to address these ethical considerations to ensure the responsible development and deployment of robotics and AI technologies.

Future Directions

As technology continues to advance, the future of robotics and AI is full of promise and endless possibilities. One of the most significant potential developments is the creation of truly autonomous robots that are capable of learning and making decisions on their own. This could lead to an increase in the use of robots in various industries, from manufacturing to healthcare. There is also the potential for AI systems and robots to collaborate and work together efficiently. Through advanced coordination and communication, robots and AI systems can perform complex tasks more effectively. This could lead to significant advancements in fields such as space exploration, disaster response, and environmental monitoring. In the future, we can also expect to see the integration of robotics and AI with other emerging technologies, such as Augmented Reality and Virtual Reality. This could lead to more immersive and interactive experiences, especially in fields like education and entertainment. Ultimately, the future of robotics and AI will depend on the efforts and contributions of engineers, innovators, and researchers in the field. With the continuous advancements in technology and growing public interest, we can expect to see more exciting developments and applications of robotics and AI in the future.

In conclusion, the field of Robotics and Artificial Intelligence presents numerous challenges and opportunities for electrical engineers. Through technological advancements, addressing ethical considerations, and exploring future directions, we can ensure the responsible and beneficial development and implementation of these technologies. As we continue to push the boundaries of what is possible, let us remember to always prioritize the ethical implications and ensure a better future for all through robotics and AI.

www.ingramcontent.com/pod-product-compliance
Lightning Source LLC
LaVergne TN
LVHW051706050326
832903LV00032B/4044